THE EXECUTIVE DIRECTOR'S SURVIVAL GUIDE

Dear Kitty,
Thanks for your help
and guidance with this
book! All the best,
Mimi

Kitty—
May you continue to
thrive in your Nonprofit
work.

THE EXECUTIVE DIRECTOR'S SURVIVAL GUIDE

THRIVING AS A NONPROFIT LEADER

Mim Carlson

Margaret Donohoe

JOSSEY-BASS
A Wiley Imprint
www.josseybass.com

Published by Jossey-Bass
A Wiley Imprint
989 Market Street, San Francisco, CA 94103-1741   www.josseybass.com

Jossey-Bass books and products are available through most bookstores. To contact Jossey-Bass directly call our Customer Care Department within the U.S. at 800-956-7739, outside the U.S. at 317-572-3986 or fax 317-572-4002.

Jossey-Bass also publishes its books in a variety of electronic formats. Some content that appears in print may not be available in electronic books.

Credit lines are on page 258.

Library of Congress Cataloging-in-Publication Data

Carlson, Mim, date.
    The executive director's survival guide: thriving as a nonprofit leader/Mim Carlson and Margaret Donohoe.—1st ed.
        p. cm.—(Jossey-Bass nonprofit and public management series)
Includes bibliographical references and index.
    ISBN 0-7879-5877-8 (alk. paper)
    1. Nonprofit organizations—Management. 2. Associations, institutions, etc.—Management. 3. Chief executive officers.
I. Donohoe, Margaret, date. II. Title. III. Series.
    HD62.6.C266   2003
    658.4'22—dc21

                                                        2003014281

Printed in the United States of America
FIRST EDITION
HB Printing   10 9 8 7 6 5 4 3 2 1

**The Jossey-Bass
Nonprofit and Public Management Series**

This book is dedicated to
Executive Directors
who have been or will be
our colleagues, clients, and mentors.

Thank you for giving your hearts and souls
to making this world a better place to live.

Contents

PART ONE

Finding Your Way as Executive Director   1

CHAPTER ONE

Succeeding in This Big Job   3

What are the roles and responsibilities of an Executive Director? • What is the difference between a leader and a manager? • When should an Executive Director lead, manage, or support others?

CHAPTER TWO

Developing as an Executive Director   13

How does an Executive Director find the time for professional development, and what opportunities are available? • What is an executive coach and how does an Executive Director find one? • How does mentoring work for an Executive Director, and who makes a good mentor? • When the going gets really tough, how does an Executive Director stay inspired?

volunteers in a change process? • How soon after a new Executive Director is hired should a change process begin?

model in encouraging inclusion and diversity? • How does an Executive Director manage diversity-related conflicts in an organization?

Exhibits

Exhibits

Preface

Our society is blessed with hundreds of thousands of nonprofit, public benefit, and nongovernmental organizations, led by an incredible cadre of paid or unpaid leaders known by such varied titles as Executive Director, Chief Executive Officer, or President, depending on the size and culture of the organization.

No matter what title they assume, these individuals are passionate, committed, resourceful, and creative people. They believe that the work their organization performs makes a significant difference in the lives of those they serve. The contributions these organizations make to society provide solid evidence that clearly supports this belief.

The reality that we and many of our nonprofit colleagues see among this inspirational group of men and women is that, despite their enviable role and their tremendous contribution to society, Executive Directors tend to struggle with the complexity of the job. The paradox is that Executive Directors can make life better for others while making their own lives more difficult. Why does this happen?

Uncovering the Paradox

What we have seen in our work as Executive Directors, and what many have shared in their stories, is that Executive Directors are exposed to and must juggle countless external and internal pressures. They wrestle with the competing internal priorities of staff and volunteer development, financial management, program effectiveness, resource development, and Board relations. At the same time, they must monitor the changing nonprofit environment, form strategic partnerships, and be responsive to stakeholders' demands for accountability. With these pressures, work-life balance becomes more difficult. Executive Directors also become less resilient and may default to their comfort zone of either managing the internal day-to-day issues and challenges or leading the organization forward toward more externally focused accomplishments. Rarely has anyone the time or energy to focus effectively on both zones. They find they tend to work harder rather than smarter, and are often the last to recognize the symptoms of burnout.

Many Executive Directors don't know where to turn for support to prevent burnout or to get their most basic questions answered. Over time some begin to feel overwhelmed and distracted by the yearning for a better quality of life.

Recent studies of Executive Directors have revealed some alarming statistics. The average tenure has declined to less than six years. The majority of current Executive Directors indicated that they do not want to be an Executive Director in their next job. This data underscores the significant retention issues in holding onto leadership talent in nonprofits.

Some experts in the field suggest that new Executive Directors require at least three to five years before they can make significant achievements in an organization. If this is so, then almost half of Executive Directors leave their position prior to reaching their full potential. Not only is organizational capacity being severely compromised, the entire nonprofit sector is wasting a major resource of talent.

Don't let these statistics scare you away if you are an Executive Director or thinking of becoming one! Instead, we hope you see the challenges that Executive Directors face as a call to reform and to rally around the role of the ED. For the nonprofit sector to thrive and continue to provide important and necessary programs, we all must acknowledge the paradox. We must look for ways to help Executive Directors survive in their positions longer and ultimately help them thrive as leaders.

Finding Your Own Path to
Success as Executive Director

The nonprofit sector is awash in literature, support organizations, and academic research expounding a variety of theories about what it takes for nonprofits to succeed. They all agree that the Executive Director, whether paid or volunteer, is one of the most critical factors to an organization's success. Our premise is that an effective Executive Director is primary to nonprofit success. Without the right leader, few organizations ever truly achieve their stated mission or potential.

The Executive Director's Survival Guide was written to encourage the heart and passion that brought EDs to their leadership roles in the first place. The focus is on helping Executive Directors strengthen and further develop personal, interpersonal, and organizational effectiveness while keeping the shifting societal changes within peripheral vision. We call the book a survival guide because it attempts to map out the complex cultural and relationship-based environment that EDs must navigate and provide practical ways to deal with some of the obstacles they are most likely to face along the way.

Ultimately, we hope this book will increase Executive Directors' resilience, help them explore new ways of managing and leading their unique organizations, find their own path to personal and organizational balance, and thrive fully as nonprofit leaders.

This book differs from most other books on the market. It doesn't try to compete with the many excellent publications for Executive Directors on managing staff, working with your Board, raising money, and the like, or the insightful books that discuss the unique nature of the nonprofit sector and key benchmarks for success. As we listen to both new and seasoned Executive Directors, we hear them say again and again that simply learning specific skills and academic theory is not enough. They struggle not so much with how to do all the tasks that must be done by an Executive Director but with how to put all the pieces together, be effective, and still have time for themselves.

We understand this to mean that Executive Directors have a need to more fully comprehend and integrate multiple roles, relationships, and resources so that their specific work can take root in their organizations and their communities.

So we see the *Survival Guide* as a companion to the many excellent how-to books in the marketplace; instead of how-to, it offers practical insight, motivating quotes, wisdom and warnings, stories from the field, and answers to some of the real-life issues EDs face. It will provide insight into the emerging trends in the nonprofit sector and the important role that organizational culture plays. It is about understanding and balancing internal and external roles and relationships so as to lead more inclusively. It is about building community and managing resources. It is about encouraging and managing organizational and personal change. It is about helping Executive Directors find their own way as nonprofit leaders.

Who This Book Is For

First and foremost, the *Survival Guide* is for Executive Directors. We wrote the book for all EDs—those new to the field, those who are already familiar with the questions raised on these pages but look for encouragement or new tools to bring to their role, and those who are struggling with their role and evaluating the decision to stay or move on to their next career.

The *Survival Guide* is also for consultants, technical assistance providers, funders, and Board members who work with Executive Directors and find themselves pondering the same questions, or looking for additional resources to support and rejuvenate the Executive Directors they work with.

Finally, the book is for anyone who has ever contemplated becoming an Executive Director. The *Survival Guide* gives a realistic picture of life as a nonprofit leader. As you will see, it is an extraordinary job for extraordinary people.

How To Get the Most from This Book

Throughout the book we will use the terms *nonprofits* or *organizations* and *Executive Directors* or *EDs* as inclusive terms for the sector and its leadership.

We use a question-and-answer format for each chapter. The questions are practical ones that have been raised by new as well as experienced Executive Directors. The answers are designed to be quickly assimilated into the day-to-day work of an ED.

Stories are scattered throughout most chapters to illustrate a variety of responses to complex issues. While some of the stories are based on our own experience, others reflect the journeys of colleagues and clients. To respect their confidentiality and candor, we have allowed the organizations and the people to remain anonymous.

Some chapters have practical materials that Executive Directors can use for themselves and for their own organizations. You will find useful tips scattered throughout the chapters that emphasize key messages. At the end of the book, a set of resource guides for each chapter will help you explore the various topics further if you so desire.

The book is divided into parts to make it easy for readers to move to the topic that most interests them. Since most Executive Directors have little time for contemplative reading, this *Survival Guide* encourages you to go quickly to the chapter or topic where you need assistance and find the specific help you want.

Part One provides a foundation to help EDs address the ultimate question: How to succeed and thrive on the job. Included is information about the essential roles and responsibilities, the characteristics required to be successful, the ways to broaden one's skills, and last but not least, the way to maintain some semblance of personal and professional balance. If you skip over this section initially, please come back.

Part Two starts by examining the importance that culture plays in creating the roles and relationships that define each organization. The next two chapters emphasize the ED's leadership role in creating a shared vision and determining effectiveness. While these topics have growing relevance to the business and government sector, they are part of the basic premise of the nonprofit sector. If your organization has lost sight of the underlying impact of its culture, or its vision, or of how to measure its success and accountability, you will find helpful information here.

Part Three explores the emerging trends facing the nonprofit sector, the changing nature of organizations as they move through their life cycle, and the ED's role in embracing changes necessary to keep an organization responsive and viable. Turn to this section if you find yourself leading an organization with systems, roles, and programs that are no longer in sync with the community or broader nonprofit sector.

Part Four focuses on the importance of building and maintaining a vast array of internal relationships. Go to this section if you are working to build, understand, or repair relationships. For an Executive Director, nothing is more important than formulating excellent relationships with Board, staff, and volunteers. And since the influence of the person who started or defined an organization is often so strong and prevalent in nonprofits, we have devoted a chapter to Founders alone. Many of the topics in this chapter can be shared with staff and Board as a way to strengthen these partnerships, which are critical to the success of Executive Directors.

Part Five discusses the role of external stakeholders, partnerships, and broad representation as the foundation for creating community to achieve the organization's mission. In these chapters you will find insight into the benefits and barriers inherent in acquiring and nurturing stakeholders, building strategic partnerships, and the varied viewpoints of multicultural organizations.

In Part Six we move into the practical demands for resources wizardry. Turn to these pages if you want some quick ideas on balancing the business or financial side of the organization, and if you want to develop a team-based approach to fundraising.

Finally, Part Seven raises the emotional yet often-overlooked subject of your own career transition. Although many nonprofits would like their Executive Director to stay forever, long tenures (fifteen years or more) are rarely healthy for the organization. If either you or your organization is feeling stagnant, this last section will prove timely.

Whatever section you turn to for support in your job, enjoy it, learn from it, and remember that, as an Executive Director, you have chosen one of the most rewarding and challenging careers.

Share Your Stories

We recognize that a significant percentage of an Executive Director's job is listening to others in order to understand their needs and expectations. This book is our gift to you. We are committed to listening to your needs and experiences. We hope you will continue to share your stories, your insights, your successes, your questions, and your challenges with us. You can reach us at info@edsurvivalguide.org—and we look forward to hearing from you!

July 2003

Mim Carlson
Kensington, California

Margaret Donohoe
San Jose, California

Acknowledgments

It takes a village to raise a child, lead a nonprofit organization, and compose a book worthy of the nonprofit sector. Many people made this book possible, and all deserve special recognition.

We appreciate the guidance, patience, and excitement for the project that Dorothy Hearst, Senior Editor at Jossey-Bass, has given us. From the early concepts and evolving focus, she has been a consistent voice for the need for this type of book.

This book has been enriched by the creative thinking, compelling questions, solid reasoning, and brilliant editing of Judi MacMurray. We are indebted to the tireless hours she gave in helping us to create the *Executive Director's Survival Guide.*

Another individual who made significant contributions is Elizabeth Norton-Schaffer, financial guru extraordinaire, who wrote the chapter on financial management. Our own efforts at this topic would never have matched her wisdom and insights.

Cindy Loveland's breadth of experience in the nonprofit sector was invaluable in identifying and screening the valuable resources you will find for each chapter at the end of the book.

Numerous individuals read early drafts and gave us their counsel and wisdom. We are grateful to Emily Goldfarb, Tim Wolfred, Kathleen Quinlan, Donna Wilson, Anna Cwieka, Pam Van Orden, Lynn Myhal, Marge Lantor, Lisa Breen Strickland, Robert Freiri, Patty Wipfler, Roni Posner, Jeannie Labozetta, Amari Romero Vorwerk, Kathi Gwynn, Barry Posner, Kitty Lopez, Molly Pollidoroff, Jane Dies, Terry Temkin, Kimberly Hsieh, Carol Evans, and Katherine Hatcher for making the *Survival Guide* a more powerful resource for Executive Directors.

Countless Executive Directors provided the framework for questions and the responses that you see in the book. Our heartfelt thanks go to Katherine Toy, Holly Van Houten, Jane Hammoud, and Mandi Billinge—and to the many other Executive Directors we have met and supported.

And last but not least we thank our respective husbands, Bob and Dennis, our families, and our animal companions for their support and encouragement throughout the journey.

The Authors

Mim Carlson and Margaret Donohoe have focused their experience, insight, and energy on helping the new generation of nonprofit leaders navigate the many opportunities and challenges of this career choice. The insight they provide is not just academic or theoretical—it comes from their own careers in the sector. They each draw on over twenty years of hands-on experience as Executive Directors, interim Executive Directors, and Board members, as well as in a variety of other leadership positions, to inform the content of the *Survival Guide.*

Mim Carlson consults and coaches in the area of organizational leadership with nonprofit organizations. She has worked for small community-based groups as well as large national nonprofits. In these organizations, she has served as an Executive Director and in other leadership positions. As a consultant, Mim specializes in Board and Executive Director development, staff leadership transitions, strategic planning, and team building. She also works as an Interim Executive Director in nonprofits that are without a person in this critical position on a permanent basis. She is the author of two books, *Winning Grants Step by Step* and *Team-Based Fundraising Step by Step,* both published by Jossey-Bass.

Margaret Donohoe guides both large and small nonprofit organizations through the opportunities and challenges of leadership, Board, and organizational transitions. Her experience as an Executive Director, active participation on a variety of nonprofit Boards and task forces, MBA from Santa Clara University, and professional development in areas of critical importance to the sector have provided her with a broad foundation of skills and insight to help Executive Directors, Boards, and their organizations not just survive but thrive in these changing times.

PART ONE

Finding Your Way as Executive Director

> *The leader beyond the millennium will not be the leader who has learned the lessons of how to do.... The leader of today and the future will be focused on how to be ... how to develop quality, character, mind-set, values, principles and courage.*
>
> —FRANCES HESSELBEIN

A CAREER IN THE NONPROFIT SECTOR equates to an unspoken calling for many. You have a strong desire to make your community and world a little better or brighter. You are driven to explore the good as well as the bad that humankind has to offer. You want to manifest your lifelong focus and interest—your vocation—to the benefit of others.

Wrapped around these qualities is a new breed of servant-leader, manager, visionary, change agent, relationship builder, and resource wizard.

The nonprofit CEO—the Executive Director—is someone who appears to effortlessly juggle multiple responsibilities, relationships, and stakeholder interests while keeping both eyes fixed on the mission and bottom line.

The reality is that nonprofit leadership is one of the most personally rewarding yet professionally complex career opportunities to be

1

found. It is not for the weak of heart. Those looking to leave behind the politics of government work or the changing economic whims of the business sector will find no safe haven here. As a colleague recently paraphrased the old saying, "The ED job isn't rocket science; it is much harder than that. Rocket science at least comes with precise formulas, mathematics and laws of physics that result in a visible outcome."

Can any Executive Director handle all these important tasks effectively and still hope to have a life beyond the nonprofit? We believe that the answer is yes, and the chapters in Part One uncover some of the answers. In Chapter One we take a close look at the unique job of the Executive Director and identify the characteristics critical to doing your job well. Chapter Two offers ways for Executive Directors to increase their effectiveness through professional development—and find the time to do so. Chapter Three offers insights and possibilities for leading a balanced life as an Executive Director. We know this is an unheard-of concept for many of you, but we believe wholeheartedly that a balanced life is possible!

CHAPTER ONE

Succeeding in This Big Job

Leaders at all levels and in all situations must pay close attention to situations in which their most effective option is to follow. . . . Because performance requires them to rely on the capacities and insights of other people.

—Douglas K. Smith,
"The Following Part of Leading," *Leader of the Future*

Executive Directors have a very big job! If you are currently working as an Executive Director, or have done so in the past, you surely know just how big and complex the position is. You converse with funders and donors, inspire and manage staff, keep Board members informed and involved, listen to clients, raise money, review (and often worry about) finances, articulate the case for your programs and the organization's accomplishments, and often serve as an accidental technology expert, facilities manager, or HR specialist, and sometimes you even clean the office. Your responsibilities seem to change depending on who needs what. You must be able to prioritize a variety of stakeholders in a multitude of different ways.

Because of all these responsibilities, Executive Directors must lead, manage, and support (follow others) to be successful. We believe that by knowing when to be a

Wisdom

The over-arching role of the Executive Director is to be caretaker of the nonprofit.

3

leader, manager, or supporter, you can more efficiently focus your efforts, and in many cases delegate to others. As a result you can make more time for a life beyond the nonprofit. In this chapter, we answer these questions:

- What are the roles and responsibilities of an Executive Director?
- What is the difference between a leader and a manager?
- When should an Executive Director lead, manage, or support others?

What are the roles and responsibilities of an Executive Director?

All Executive Directors (paid or unpaid) share one universal role, regardless of where they work. The Board always hires the ED as a temporary caretaker of the mission, entrusting the organization to the ED with the expectation that it will thrive in that person's care. So the Executive Director neither owns nor controls the nonprofit, but is responsible for making it thrive.

To perform this central caretaker role, an Executive Director must have five important characteristics. The strength of each will differ from person to person, but every Executive Director needs some combination of all of the following:

- Visionary
- Change agent
- Relationship builder
- Community creator
- Resource wizard

These characteristics will look different in each person, and in each nonprofit. In some nonprofits, all five characteristics may need to be in evidence all the time, while in others they ebb and flow in the Executive Director depending on the needs of the organization.

Throughout the remainder of the book, we will be describing these characteristics in great detail and offering you ideas on how to apply them in your nonprofit. First, though, to understand them more fully, it's helpful to look at the five characteristics in terms of the Executive Director's responsibilities.

The characteristics of an Executive Director are manifested and become apparent in the responsibilities of the position. These responsibilities generally are listed in the job description or work plan for the ED. They vary from person to person and nonprofit to nonprofit, depending on the size and culture of the organization and where it is in its life cycle. Exhibit 1.1 highlights the key responsibilities of an Executive Director and should be viewed as an illustration of what most EDs are responsible for in most organizations. You may find it helpful to use this chart to create a more specific list of responsibilities for you in your own nonprofit.

Wisdom

Every Executive Director has key responsibilities that relate to being a visionary, change agent, relationship builder, community builder, and resource wizard.

Exhibit 1.1 Responsibilities of an Executive Director

As a *visionary,* an Executive Director is responsible for

- Motivating internal and external stakeholders with a shared picture of the greatness of their nonprofit.

- Inspiring passion to achieve what is possible.

- Bringing focus to the vision with a strategic plan.

- Thinking strategically about the best way to meet community needs.

- Evaluating, on an ongoing basis, the effectiveness of the nonprofit in fulfilling its mission.

As a *change agent,* an Executive Director is responsible for

- Keeping aware of trends in the nonprofit sector to ensure the organization remains responsive to changing community needs, shifting revenue sources, emerging competition, and ever-increasing public scrutiny.

- Monitoring the nonprofit's internal changes and providing the skills needed to lead, manage, and support the organization at any point in its life cycle.

Exhibit 1.1 Responsibilities of an Executive Director (continued)

- Managing internal change processes by working with stakeholders to set goals and outcomes, create plans, and make the change happen.

- Persuading and motivating others to accept change as part of the daily routine in the organization, while also acknowledging people's natural resistance to change.

- Taking risks to try new ideas and take new approaches to achieving the mission.

As a *relationship builder,* an Executive Director is responsible for

- Communicating successfully with internal stakeholders—staff, volunteers, and Board.

- Managing staff and volunteers in a manner that fosters a healthy culture to ensure that everyone's role on the team is valued and recognized.

- Supporting and at times leading the Board of Directors to ensure they add value to the organization.

- Carrying the wisdom of the organization's Founder while implementing bold new ideas.

As a *community creator,* the Executive Director is responsible for

- Creating a visible organization with broad stakeholder support.

- Communicating with external stakeholders to ensure continuing interest and involvement in the mission.

- Building partnerships that further the mission through cooperative efforts and strategic relationships.

- Valuing diversity and creating an organizational culture that appreciates and respects differences.

As a *resource wizard,* an Executive Director is responsible for

- Recruiting, mentoring, and recognizing people who will raise funds that allow the organization to thrive.

- Communicating and building relationships with funders and donors to gain interest in the mission and support for it.

- Stewarding and managing funds received so well that the organization's trustworthiness is unquestionable.

The list of responsibilities in the exhibit may seem like a long one to anyone who has not experienced the job of an Executive Director. The list is long, particularly when you think about the specific tasks needed for each responsibility. Remember, though, that not all responsibilities have highest priority on any given day.

In some smaller organizations that have no paid staff, the Executive Director may struggle to accomplish any of the indicated responsibilities because of the need to handle routine tasks normally performed by others in larger organizations. In this case, an ED needs to remember the core responsibilities as listed here, and work diligently to delegate as much of the other work as possible to volunteers.

Being a successful Executive Director is a learned role—no one starts out in the position as the "perfect ED." In fact, successful Executive Directors are always improving themselves and taking time to build and strengthen the skills most needed to fulfill their responsibilities and lead their nonprofit to greater success. Remember this if you find yourself doubting your capabilities or feeling inadequate. The very big job of an Executive Director requires an ongoing process of learning and development.

WARNING

Don't view this big job of Executive Director as yours alone to handle. Freely ask for support or advice; if you insist on doing everything yourself, people may let you try—and that will be a disaster for everyone.

What is the difference between a leader and a manager?

These days people constantly speak and write about leadership and management styles. How often have you heard someone described as "a great leader but a weak manager" or "a great manager of people but not a very good leader"? What do those comments mean? The lines between the definitions of *manager* and *leader* have blurred to the point that people often use the words interchangeably. But being a successful manager and being a great leader are two very different roles—and both are required of Executive Directors on a daily basis if they are to fulfill the broader role of caretaker for the organization.

The challenge is twofold: knowing the difference between leadership and management, and discerning when to use one or the other.

A *manager* focuses attention on efficiency, effectiveness, and making sure the right things happen at the right time. This is an essential role for every Executive Director.

You are in a manager role when you set performance objectives with staff, prepare budgets, review cash flow projections, develop action plans, and evaluate programs or fundraising strategies or any other aspect of the nonprofit. Managing may also include doing hundreds of other tasks that require focused and logical attention to the good health of the organization.

On the other hand, a *leader* is a strategist, a visionary, and someone who inspires others to greatness. This is also a critical role for Executive Directors in any organization. You are leading when you share your vision for your nonprofit, or when you bring staff and volunteers together to design a program or develop a strategy or resolve a problem. Leaders motivate staff and volunteers, serve as role models, inspire donors to give generously, build community and capacity inside and outside the nonprofit, and create learning environments in which people can grow and develop themselves without fear. A strong leader will display all of the characteristics discussed in this chapter.

One of our Executive Director colleagues expressed the difference between leader and manager this way: *"When you are a leader, you work from the heart. As a manager, you work from the head."* Although it is probably more complex than that, the point to remember is the difference between what you do as a leader and what you do as a manager—and the constant need to be able to do both. Furthermore, the head and heart need to be partners, not independent operators.

When should an Executive Director lead, manage, or support others?

Executive Directors generally understand they have the roles of leading and managing in the nonprofit. Supporting others and following their lead is sometimes more challenging. There seems to be an unwritten rule that new Executive Directors absorb through their pores—that to be a good Executive Director, you always have to be in charge and responsible for every aspect of the organization. You can throw that out the window now, because it just isn't true. As a matter of fact, the best and most successful Executive Directors are those that seek out and develop leadership and management qualities in paid and unpaid staff and Board members. In addition, they enjoy empowering others, giving them the responsibility and authority to lead the organization. By supporting paid and unpaid staff and Board members, you can try on new ideas, learn new practices, and grow as an Executive Director. At the same time, you will give others the opportunity to take leadership or management roles, to be innovative, and to grow into their own personal style, deepening your organization's leadership reserves so you can concentrate on the parts of your job that matter most—and even develop the breathing room to take some time off.

Wisdom

A supporting role for you is one way to ensure the organization has strong leadership after your departure. This is perhaps your ultimate responsibility as caretaker.

To discern when to lead, manage, or support, think about your role as ED as outlined in Exhibit 1.2 on page 11.

The lists in the exhibit are not exhaustive and will of course be different for each Executive Director. The main point is that no one person, not even you, can single-handedly juggle all of the required activities effectively. Your primary responsibility to your nonprofit is leadership, and that leadership must include the wisdom to know when to become a manager and a supporter. You must know when to seek out and ask for help and when to take time to develop support that will ensure success for you, your nonprofit, and the community you serve. The following "Story from the Field" illustrates this point.

After graduating from college with a degree in sociology (and a desire to save the world!), Mim applied for her first Executive Director's job at a family health community clinic in Texas. In the interview, she was told that the ten staff people worked together as a collective with equal rights and equal pay, and they only gave anyone the title of Executive Director because federal family planning contracts mandated it. Bravely, she accepted the position and quickly became immersed in issues of authority, decision making, communication, and control.

Mim understood that the clinic needed a manager who could achieve the level of efficiency required by federal contracts. On a much more vague level she understood that the clinic needed a leader who had a vision and could inspire its independent-minded and passionate people.

Mim began her work at the clinic believing that as an Executive Director, she was in charge of everything, responsible for everything and everyone, and of course had little room for mistakes! To follow someone else's lead might be counterproductive, and might in fact badly mess things up for her.

The toughest lesson was recognizing that leadership sometimes includes being a follower or supporter. Because this was a collective of equals, Mim quickly had to learn that effectiveness as a manager and a leader depended on her willingness to be a follower—to let other staff people take the lead with their ideas. It was frightening at first, especially when she found herself clashing with a few of these capable people. The result was an atmosphere of increasing mistrust, disrespect, and internal bickering. Mim began to see how her belief that she had to be in charge of everything was leading to disaster for everyone.

Mim was not the only leader in the nonprofit. Staff, volunteers, Board members, and community stakeholders all knew more than she did about certain aspects of the organization or had expertise in areas where she definitely lacked proficiency. The creative and innovative people around her had great ideas that they were quite capable of implementing.

Fortunately, Mim recognized the value of these resources before it was too late. She saw the fallacies of her initial perceptions of what a good Executive Director was and learned the value of supporting and following. Her relationships with staff improved and she became a much more effective leader and manager as the staff progressed toward a collective shared vision.

Exhibit 1.2 Executive Director as Leader, Manager, Supporter

You *lead* when your nonprofit needs direction and focus for relationships that create unity within the nonprofit and stronger communities outside, an inspiring vision to generate passion and excitement, resources that support and enhance success, increased capacity to fulfill the mission, and change to stay effective and true to the community.

You *manage* when the nonprofit needs tactical plans to keep programs on track and funds coming in, processes and procedures to keep staff and volunteers accountable, budgets and finance reports to ensure sustainability, and written materials to promote the organization and satisfy stakeholders.

You *support and follow the lead of others* when your nonprofit has Board, staff, or volunteers interested and skilled (or willing to develop skills) in building and sustaining relationships, planning and carrying out programs, making the organization visible, ensuring financial stability and growth, managing internal changes, or tracking external trends.

Learning when to take the support role is important and sometimes difficult for many Executive Directors. Conversely, it is also important to discern who not to follow. Following individuals who do not display the leadership characteristics we described earlier in this chapter, or people who are generally not valued by those in your organization, is a clear prescription for trouble. Taking time to assess these leadership indicators can prove invaluable.

Believing that the Executive Director always has to know the right thing to do in any situation is guaranteed to make the job more difficult than it already is. It's an unfair expectation that too many Executive Directors put on themselves, to the ultimate detriment of everyone.

Wisdom

Supporting others in the organization to take a leadership role is healthy and in no way diminishes or threatens your own leadership role.

Very often, the best leadership practice is to identify knowledgeable, trustworthy individuals to whom you can delegate and then follow them.

The big job of being an Executive Director has its challenges with the overall role of caretaker, and the numerous responsibilities assigned to it. However, the rewards you receive often far outweigh these challenges. Under your care, the nonprofit's programs, staff, Board, and community can thrive. Your own growth as a leader, manager, and supporter can also be viewed as a huge reward on both a personal and professional level.

CHAPTER TWO

Developing as an Executive Director

Apart from learning from books and experiences, leaders learn by self-reflection. . . . They also learn from mentors. . . . Most of all, they learn by personal experimentation, often putting themselves in challenging situations that require tenacity, courage, and personal growth.
—BURT NANUS AND STEPHEN DOBBS,
Leaders Who Make a Difference

EXECUTIVE DIRECTORS, like all leaders, need development opportunities to inspire them and keep them in touch with the best practices of their profession. This chapter addresses the following questions that Executive Directors ask about ways to develop themselves:

- How does an Executive Director find the time for professional development, and what opportunities are available?
- What is an executive coach and how does an Executive Director find one?
- How does mentoring work for an Executive Director, and who makes a good mentor?
- When the going gets really tough, how does an Executive Director stay inspired?

How does an Executive Director find the time for professional development, and what opportunities are available?

Part of the answer to this question involves time management, and balancing and prioritizing your workload to include time for professional development. Most Executive Directors know this is important, but for various reasons, self-development never makes it to the top of the priority list. We recommend you put this task right up at the top with your other key priorities. Here are some ideas of what you can do to make time for professional development:

- Include in your work plan each year ways you want to develop professionally, and budget funds for them.
- Discuss your professional development ideas with your Board Chair or Executive Committee, and obtain their commitment to supporting you.
- Make staff development a norm of the organization's culture so that all staff have a priority of growing in their position.
- Plan far in advance for classes, conferences, and other activities, trying to find those that occur during times when your organization's activity level is likely to be relatively low.
- Take the necessary time to reflect on what you learned and envision ways to apply your new knowledge to your work.

Wisdom

Professional development is an essential component to successful leadership. It should be a high priority of every Executive Director.

These are simple, basic time management ideas that will work if you have a commitment to professional development. But what happens if you have done everything right to find the time necessary, and in spite of your best efforts an unexpected crisis looms over your organization on the day you have committed to a development activity for yourself?

When that happens (as it probably will), ask yourself these two questions:

Is this a life-or-death crisis for the organization? If it is, you need to immediately address the crisis, and then reschedule—not cancel—the development activity. If the crisis is not life-threatening, you can inform significant people of its nature and define the steps that you will take after the professional development activity is over. Or you can find individuals to step in and handle the crisis for you while you are gone—enhancing their development in the process.

Is this a leadership crisis or a management one? If it's a management crisis, then someone on the staff or the Board or among the volunteer force can probably handle the crisis until you return. If it is a leadership crisis, then you may need to shift priorities until that crisis is met.

Remember that it is very important to bring Board members into any leadership crisis, both to keep them informed and to obtain their help in ending it. Board members should also be involved in any shifting of ED-level priorities so that their expectations of you are kept up to date.

Executive Directors interested in professional development have endless activities to choose from. Exhibit 2.1 lists some of the more popular ones, but is not exhaustive. To find interesting and relevant opportunities in your area, contact related professional associations, Chambers of Commerce, local nonprofit management support organizations, and national groups such as the Alliance for Nonprofit Management (available online at http://www.allianceonline.org/).

Depending on your budget size, you can pick and choose from an endless catalogue of development activities. Some, like participating in an informal ED support group, generally don't cost money. Others, such as attending a conference, may be more expensive and may stretch budget resources. The critical point to understand is that the growth and long-term health of your organization require commitment to the ongoing growth and development of its leadership. An Executive Director who actively participates in professional development is essential to sustainable organization growth.

Wisdom

No matter how long you have been in the profession or how skilled you are as an Executive Director, there are learning opportunities for you and new discoveries to be made.

Exhibit 2.1 Professional Development
Activities for Executive Directors

- Look for workshops and conferences related to your various roles:

  Management-related workshops on budgeting, supervision, fundraising, strategic planning, and numerous other topics

  Leadership development workshops on team building, Board–ED partnership development, diversity in the workplace, or community partnerships

  Conferences sponsored by local or regional nonprofit management assistance organizations, where you can network and share experiences and resources with other professionals in your field

- Find an ED support group and attend regularly.

- Find a mentor or coach to work with you.

- Enroll in a college or university nonprofit certificate or degree program. Some of these are online programs and easier to handle for the time-crunched executive.

- Conduct Web searches for books and articles related to ED professional development. Then take time to obtain and read them!

What is an executive coach and how does an Executive Director find one?

The concept of having a coach is relatively new to nonprofits. The corporate sector has seen the value of executive coaches for several years, and more and more nonprofits are turning to this pool of talent for their leaders.

Many Executive Directors are somewhat unclear about what a coach is, and what that person does. Adding to the confusion, people who talk about coaching may be referring to one of many models:

- Mentor coach
- Co-active coach

- Work team coach
- Performance coach
- Systems coach

And even that list isn't complete; you'll hear of still other types of coaches that work with individuals and entire organizations. Since this book is about you, the Executive Director, this section will just focus on individual coaching.

Coaches are people who encourage and support executives while guiding them to make powerful changes in their lives. The International Coaching Federation (ICF) has established ethical guidelines for coaches that further describe the person and the work, maintaining that coaches believe in the dignity and integrity of every human being and remain committed to eliciting the inherent capability and resourcefulness of every individual. The coach's proper approach, the guidelines point out, is to use an interactive process to help clients develop strategies and solutions that help them toward the rapid attainment of their goals. A coach is "respectful and protective of the vulnerability of each client," while at the same time holding each client to "a high standard of self-responsibility and accountability" and maintaining a personal standard of objectivity and competence. The overall goal is to practice in the best interests of the client, the community, and society.

Having a coach who practices within the guidelines of the ICF can add tremendous value for an Executive Director. A coach can

- Guide you to manage your work and life changes more effectively.
- Extend your wisdom through mentoring.
- Help you to stay focused and set priorities.
- Work with you to clarify values, purpose, and direction both at work and in life.

Wisdom

Support from a coach, mentor, or peer makes the big job of an Executive Director more doable and provides camaraderie to lessen the loneliness at the top.

- Encourage personal empowerment.
- Tease out new perspectives that result in your transformation.

It is also important to understand what coaches will not do for you. They are not psychotherapists. They are concerned about your present and future life, not your past. Coaches are also not problem solvers, though by working with a coach, you will solve many problems. The coach's job is to support you as you find your own solutions to problems. This may be done through mentoring, or by challenging your theories, or with another method of facilitating your learning. Coaches are also not agenda-driven; they focus instead on helping you to create your own agenda and be responsible for it.

So how do you know if a coach is right for you? A good start is to answer the following four questions:

- Do you want a change in your life, for instance, to become more conscious or competent in some area?
- Are you willing to think beyond your own mind-sets or mental models to explore new perspectives?
- Are you willing to look deeply inside yourself at your values, beliefs, personal strengths, and limitations?
- Are you curious about what possibilities your future may hold? Can you be open to dreaming about and visioning those possibilities for yourself?

If your answers are all yes and you want to find a professional coach, or if you just want more information about coaching, check out the Web sites of these three organizations: The Coaches Training Institute, the Professional Coaches and Mentors Association, and the International Coaches Federation. All three are listed in the Recommended Resources for this chapter. Local management service organizations are also becoming a source on nonprofit-specific coaching.

One criticism we often hear about hiring a coach is the expense involved. Coaches may charge $200 to $300 a month for two to four hours of work with you. While the price may seem high to some, most people report that the value of having a coach work one-on-one with them far outweighs the cost.

Story from the Field

A very busy Executive Director of a nonprofit serving youth began her coaching session by reporting that she was burned out and ready to quit. As the Founder of the group, she felt she carried the organization on her shoulders and was isolated from her Board and staff. After just one session she could see new possibilities for engaging others to work more closely with her, while also establishing new boundaries on her availability. As her coaching continued, she began leaving work at a consistently reasonable hour and engaging in a few other stress-reducing activities that enabled her to work with new energy, not to mention enjoy herself more. Was the cost of coaching worth it for her?—Of course!

An alternative to having an individual coach is to join a peer group or leadership circle. Most of the groups we are familiar with are geared to professional development and are an excellent resource for learning and growing in the profession. They are, of course, also good for networking. The groups often meet in person on a regular basis, and some conference-call peer groups are being formed for busy professionals who struggle to leave the office.

Warning

Never let your passion for the mission of your organization die. Give yourself breathing room to reinvigorate, reenergize, and recommit yourself to it.

Sometimes, a peer group will develop for Executive Directors of mission-similar organizations, such as environmental nonprofits or youth services. Other groups are formed with Executive Directors from different backgrounds in order to gain a broader perspective.

The value of belonging to a peer group is that you have structured time to talk about achievements, problems, new learning, and other important topics. You receive support from individuals who have hands-on experience with situations like the ones that are new to you and can give you ideas, reality checks, a sounding board, or a vehicle for safely venting frustration. Belonging to a support group is also a great way to reduce that lonely-at-the-top feeling reported by many Executive Directors.

Finding an Executive Director peer group in your community can be challenging. If you have an organization in your community that provides training or other technical assistance to nonprofits, that's usually a good place to start. These organizations may have already formed a peer group for Executive Directors or may know of some that exist in the community. Sometimes funders will know of Executive Director peer groups as well. Word of mouth is often the most reliable source of information. Call other Executive Directors in your area and find out if they know of any peer groups. If your efforts to locate an existing group fail, then perhaps you can use your leadership skills to get one formed!

How does mentoring work for an Executive Director, and who makes a good mentor?

Almost everyone has had a mentor at some point. Mentors are people who are trusted and respected for their wisdom. They are teachers and guides. A mentor for an Executive Director is someone who models the leadership skills and qualities that you aspire to have for yourself.

As the executive coaching field gains popularity, confusion sometimes arises over the differences between a mentor and a coach. Some people use the words synonymously, while others believe differences exist. For the purposes of this book, we define a *mentor* as someone with similar experience to yours and with whom you have an informal relationship. Your mentor may offer advice or challenge you to take on unfamiliar job tasks with their assistance to guide you. By contrast, you have a formal relationship with your coach, whom you employ to help you identify specific ways to grow professionally and to coach you toward meeting those goals.

Sometimes, you will know your mentor. The person may be a former colleague or boss, or a current teacher. Sometimes your mentors will come from history, be famous, or distant and not even know the role they play for you. Other people are directly asked to serve as mentors for a period of time. Mentors can inspire you, and can help you as an Executive Director to

- Make good, sound decisions.
- Increase your knowledge of the profession.
- Gain focus and perspective.
- Solve problems.

Some of these may sound similar to the values provided by coaches, and indeed there are many similarities between the two professions. In fact, your coach may also be your mentor if you've been fortunate enough to find someone who has significant knowledge as an Executive Director and holds qualities that you value.

Finding a mentor is easy. Just look around at Executive Directors you admire and would like to emulate. Or find former Executive Directors who are now consultants or working in some other profession, or are retired. Once you identify a potential mentor, ask this person to mentor you for a period of time, and describe why you made this choice. Most people feel flattered and honored to be asked to be a mentor.

When the going gets really tough, how does an Executive Director stay inspired?

It is not unusual to find an Executive Director who is feeling overwhelmed and losing all inspiration for the job. When individuals tell us they are losing their passion, focus, inspiration, or whatever word they use to describe an essential quality of job connection, we immediately wonder what barrier has developed. Have job pressures gotten in the way? Is the struggle for funding just too much to handle right now? Have external or internal criticisms reduced self-esteem? Has there been a loss of personal purpose? All these factors and many more can cause a loss of inspiration.

More than people in any other profession, Executive Directors take on this difficult job because of some passion or inspiration that sustains them through good times and bad. When you feel your passion and inspiration, you feel alive, energetic, and productive. By contrast, when a barrier comes between you and your passion and inspiration, you can feel overwhelmed, lethargic, guilty, bored, or just plain negative.

We cannot emphasize enough the importance of taking time to reflect on what lies beneath this loss of inspiration. It is equally important to ask yourself what you need to regain that passion. Since these questions may clearly be easier to ask than to answer, a beginning strategy for coping with that sense of "it just doesn't matter anymore" is to get up from your desk—even in the middle of a busy, chaotic day—especially when you feel like you are crumbling under the weight of some huge burden—and break away for even a few minutes. Dare to take a fifteen-minute walk around the block or spend an even longer period of time in a park or garden—remove yourself from interaction with the immediate job circumstances. We know of one Executive Director who takes naps to regain inspiration!

Here are some other ideas on ways to pinpoint the barriers to your inspiration and begin to regain it:

- Take yourself on a day-long retreat with an agenda that has you answering the questions like these:

  What inspires me?

  What is blocking my ability to be inspired?

  What can I do to remove those barriers?

What can I ask others to do to help me remove them?

What will keep me inspired today, tomorrow, and in the future?

- Have a staff retreat where people can talk about what inspires, motivates, and empowers them. Share your own thoughts, and benefit from the group's inspiration.

- Take some time (an hour or whatever you can afford) to focus on your vision for your organization. Is the vision still inspiring to you or is it time to revisit it and make it bolder?

- Find a mentor or coach to support you and help you rediscover your inspiration.

- Give yourself recognition for being an incredible person doing an amazing job that is making a difference. If you are unable to give yourself recognition, then find someone to do it for you.

- Form a personal Board of Directors or Advisory Council that is filled with people who have shared your passion and vision, and are inspired by many of the things you are. Go to them when you find yourself drained of inspiration and let them fill you back up.

Chapter Eighteen returns to this point, offering further thoughts on reconnecting with your passion as well as considering whether it's time for a new career.

CHAPTER THREE

Finding Balance in the Role of Executive Director

Have fun in your command.

Don't always run at breakneck pace.

Take time when you've earned it and spend time with your family.

Surround yourself with people who take their work seriously, but not themselves.

—GENERAL COLIN POWELL

MUCH HAS BEEN WRITTEN about balance and how elusive that goal is for Executive Directors. The job of an ED is composed of numerous and ever-changing roles and responsibilities. You are required to be accountable to a complex, diverse, and often demanding array of stakeholders from your Board of Directors to your funders. In addition, there is seldom enough staff or volunteer help to accomplish all that needs to be done. As a result, balance tends to seem out of reach, leading to personal burnout for the Executive Director—and paralysis for an entire organization.

Are any of the following classic signs of being overstressed or burned out familiar to you?

- Difficulty making decisions
- Negative feelings about people you work with

- Loneliness at the top
- Avoidance of tasks that need to be done
- Feeling overwhelmed most of the time
- Believing you need to work days, nights, and weekends
- Fear and despair that you aren't doing a good enough job

If so, you are not alone. Balance and burnout were two of the most frequently cited challenges among the Executive Directors we interviewed prior to developing *The Executive Director's Survival Guide*. At times, all Executive Directors feel overwhelmed. It goes with the territory. But no Executive Director should allow life to become so unbalanced that symptoms of burnout make it difficult to lead effectively.

This chapter focuses on some self-reflection techniques and steps you can take to find time to lead a balanced life and still build a rewarding career as an Executive Director. The questions we will address are simple but critical to your success:

- Why are Executive Directors so susceptible to burnout?
- How can I find balance as an Executive Director?
- How do I set boundaries on my work life so I still have a personal life?
- Where do I find the time to do everything an Executive Director has to do?
- How can an Executive Director delegate when everyone is already busy?

Why are Executive Directors so susceptible to burnout?

The potential for burnout increases dramatically depending on who you are, where you work, and what your job is. Thus the road to burnout is paved with good intentions and good EDs. Most agree that if you're a hard worker who gives 110 percent, an idealistic, self-motivated achiever who thinks anything is possible if you just work hard enough, you are a possible candidate for burnout.

The same is true if you're a rigid perfectionist with unrealistically high standards and expectations. In a job with frequent people contact or deadlines, you advance from a possible to a probable candidate.

There's certainly nothing wrong with being an idealistic, hardworking perfectionist or a self-motivating achiever. There's nothing wrong with having high aspirations and expectations. Indeed, these are admirable traits most often cited in job announcements for Executive Directors.

The problem is in unrealistic job descriptions and internally driven expectations. While you may not have a lot of control over the day-to-day issues that create stress in your organization and your job, you do have control over how you respond. Thus it is important for all EDs to recognize the underlying personal and organizational sources of pressure and take conscious steps toward working with their Boards to establish realistic expectations while creating their own personal and professional balance and boundaries.

If you are susceptible to burnout or worse yet feel overwhelmed by the stress of the job, seek help. Do not isolate yourself or think it will go away. A coach or counselor can help you tease apart the various causes of stress and take steps to identify and improve upon those that are controllable.

> ## Wisdom
>
> The most effective leaders are those who manage to achieve some level of balance in their lives.

How can I find balance as an Executive Director?

Finding balance isn't a single outcome or goal, it's an ongoing process. The definition of balance is unique to each person's values and life situation. Balance is a gift you have to create for yourself; no one can do it for you.

And you must do it. An Executive Director who is consistently overwhelmed by competing priorities cannot be an effective leader. Society is rich in approaches, theories, books, and self-help seminars about the need to negotiate the increasingly complex demands of work and personal life to feel fulfilled, balanced, in control of your life and generally healthier. It takes work—and mental energy that is hard to find once you start down the slide toward burnout—to find the ones that are right for you.

A simple approach to the question of balance begins with awareness and self-reflection. It's essential to consider trade-offs between your personal values and your organization's priorities in light of your individual perception of consequences.

The following simple exercise is aimed at helping you clarify your individual values versus the reality of where you spend your time. Exhibit 3.1 will help you locate your own imbalances and explore options for juggling or negotiating balance back into your life.

Exhibit 3.1 Life Balance Reflection

Priorities	Life in Balance (*percent of total*)	Real Time Allocation (*percent of total*)	Discrepancy (*difference as percent of ideal*)
Work			
Family			
Health			
Home			
Friends			
Relationships			
Hobbies			
Professional development			

1. Using the chart in Exhibit 3.1 as a model, identify your own priorities—what you want for your life right now—and list them in the first column. They may include some of the ones in the exhibit or you may have your own unique list.

2. Envision your life as balanced, and estimate the percentage of your time you would spend on average on each of these priorities if that were the case. Place the percentages in the second column.

3. Now for a reality check. How do you really spend your time? Estimate percentages for what a typical week or month looks like, and post them in the third column.

4. Where are the greatest discrepancies between reality and balance? In the exhibit, the fourth column was calculated by taking the difference between the goal and the reality and figuring it as a percentage of the goal. Looking at the numbers may well be enough—you probably won't have to go through the math to see what you need to work on first.

5. List some realistic, small steps you could take in order to feel more satisfied and fulfilled.

6. Look at the steps you've listed. What is blocking you *right now* from taking these steps? Are these steps or changes things you have control of or do you need to negotiate some changes with your Board, your family, and your staff?

7. Think about the implications of the choices you face. What are the consequences of not taking these steps toward balance? What are the immediate and long-term rewards or benefits of greater balance?

The process of defining and achieving balance is a personal one. You have to make it a priority, set realistic goals, and do it. Everyone has some sort of barrier or blockage that stands in the way of achieving personal goals. Clearing these blockages is a significant step and may require outside support from a colleague or friend, or even a professional coach.

For instance, let's say you have decided that your life would be more balanced if you could get some exercise on a regular basis and see your friends more often. Making that determination is the easy step! You could decide to go to the gym five days a week and see friends every other evening. But could you do it? This would certainly be an unrealistic goal for most busy Executive Directors, and you would probably doom yourself to failure. Instead, you could decide to find a couple of friends to work out with, or walk with, or join you in any number of enjoyable exercise-related activities one or two days a week.

Setting some self-prescribed work boundaries will also help you gain balance in your life.

How do I set boundaries on my work life so I still have a personal life?

One key to finding balance in your life is by setting some clear boundaries and sticking to them. Establishing work boundaries is a mental activity more than anything else. Most people who become Executive Directors are highly motivated, driven by an important mission, and full of desire to succeed for the community being served. American society has produced a work ethic that measures success through how hard people work. But we have found in our work as Executive Directors (and

with them) that it isn't how hard you work that really matters. It's how smart or effectively you work. Part of working smart is allowing time on a regular basis for non–work-related activities, and believing this is okay. For most people, the most creative and strategic thoughts do not happen in the office, they come in the middle of doing something else—exercising, conversation, on vacation, reading a book.

To set new work boundaries, you may need to educate your staff and Board of Directors, persuading them that it is important to set boundaries for themselves, as well as modeling the new behavior patterns. The first step is to acknowledge that the culture of excessive hours is unhealthy and help your staff begin to move toward one that rewards new behaviors and realistic work boundaries. Many times we have heard complaints from disgruntled staff and Board members who tell us their Executive Director isn't doing the job well. The problem? The ED dares to take a lunch hour or leave the office regularly at 5 P.M. We've stopped being surprised by these comments and now spend time helping people understand why it is important for everyone to set these boundaries. In the long run, it's better for the agency because the Executive Director is not burning out and can be more effective for a longer tenure with the organization.

Story from the Field

An Executive Director of a regional senior center set a clear boundary with her Board that she needed to leave at 5 P.M. every day to pick up her child. She agreed that evening meetings were possible as long as she could spend the two hours from 5 P.M. to 7 P.M. picking up, feeding, and playing briefly with her child. The Board agreed to this and the Executive Director never made an exception. The few staff and Board members who questioned her commitment and effectiveness were quickly silenced because of the Executive Director's ability to do her job well.

Talk to your Board Chair and jointly establish some important boundaries in your work to allow you to find the balance you need to continue to be an effective leader. The boundary you set may be a schedule boundary like the one the senior center ED established, or it may be a task boundary such as only attending two evening meetings or events in a week and delegating Board members, volunteers, or staff to attend any others. If your vision of a more balanced life is related to health issues, you may need a work boundary that has you eating healthier meals in a quiet location or even negotiating a flexible or reduced work schedule to achieve or regain your vision of balance. In Chapter Ten we discuss the concept of establishing a social contract with each new Board Chair that may also help to define some professional and personal boundaries.

Where do I find the time to do everything an Executive Director has to do?

This question immediately raises the priorities flag for us and we look to see if the Executive Director has been given clear directives from the Board of Directors regarding performance priorities and expectations. Is an accepted work plan established that both the Board and ED have agreed upon? Usually, we find that the Board has failed to develop the ED's job description and has defaulted to the slogan, "Just do it." Unfortunately, that's not very specific or helpful.

So the first step toward finding time is to work with your Board of Directors to clarify and establish some jointly developed priorities. You may already have some tools to help guide this negotiation.

If you have a job description, this is a good starting point. Is it up-to-date and relevant to the job that you actually do? If not, work with your Board to update it so that it accurately reflects the job you have today, not the job you were hired into five years ago. A well-crafted job description goes a long way toward clarifying your roles and responsibilities. Some organizations will take an added step to emphasize each key area of responsibility in the job description and indicate with a percentage figure its relative importance. For example, one organization that was launching a capital campaign broke out its priorities as follows:

Administration and management	20 percent
Board of Directors	25 percent
Fund development and community relations	30 percent
Strategic planning and evaluations	25 percent

The reality was that administration and management currently accounted for about 60 percent of the ED's week. Rather than simply leave the ED to do everything and work longer hours, the Board and ED came up with a plan that promoted one of the organization's senior managers to Associate Director to take on added responsibilities for program oversight and administrative details, freeing up about ten to fifteen hours a week for the Executive Director to work on Board development, community relations, and fund development issues in order to build a strong foundation for the capital campaign. The new Associate Director thrived on the additional responsibilities.

The second place to look for clarity is the organization's strategic plan or annual goals. Whether it is a formalized plan carefully preserved in formal binders or simply summary notes from a Board meeting, it is a start. The key question for you and the Board to ask is, where do you need to focus your talents and time to help make these goals become reality?

We also encourage you to avoid one of the common weaknesses of such a discussion. That is, the outcome is a long list with fifteen to twenty so-called priorities on it. While such a list may summarize a variety of issues facing the organization, it does nothing to provide clarity, direction, and focus. Don't let a list of priorities exceed five items, and three is better. The extra step it takes to whittle the list down forces you and the Board to carefully debate and negotiate what is most important rather than everything that needs to be done. The other items should not be discarded. They may become secondary priorities once the key three to five issues are addressed. While the resulting priority list may be invaluable to you, the process or discussion the organization engages in is even more important, as it helps strengthen a unified vision and Board-ED partnership (a point discussed in more detail in Chapter Six).

WARNING

Never underestimate the importance of having a life outside of the organization.

Even after you and the Board achieve clarity in defining the Executive Director position, you may well find there is still too much for one person to do. And, because the modern environment is changing so rapidly,

new priorities emerge and need to be juggled with existing ones.

If you are feeling the pressure of competing priorities, we recommend asking yourself the following questions to help determine what issues really need *your* immediate attention. You may also want to involve others in your organization, such as key staff or volunteers and Board members.

- Which priorities are leadership-related and which are management-related? Of those that are management-related, can I delegate them to someone else to allow me to focus on the leadership priorities?

- Do I need information from someone else in order to undertake the priority? Is this person available now, or will I need to wait? If I need to wait, can I set up an appointment now so I feel I am making some progress toward achieving this priority?

- Which priorities on the list are life-and-death issues for my agency? A life-and-death issue is one that requires something to be done soon or the clients or community may be negatively affected, the agency doors will close, or resources of funding or people are lost—issues that threaten the immediate existence of the agency.

Story from the Field

One Executive Director who effectively renegotiated her priorities into a work plan with her Board did so by calling the twenty-member Board together for an evening planning session. The purpose of the planning session was to look at the growing list of agency issues and compare them with the work plan of the Executive Director that had been approved earlier that year.

The new priorities that had been added came primarily from the community. The organization is an active neighborhood association with a staff of four who listen to and speak for the neighborhood. Community members were always calling or dropping by and asking the Executive Director to please take care of something that was bothering them. As you can imagine, the to-do list became huge very quickly and the Executive Director began feeling pressure from her Board and the community to meet everyone's priorities.

At the planning session, the Board looked at the original work plan and the growing list from the community. Together with the staff, they determined which priorities were most related to the mission and long-range goals of the organization, which priorities were do-or-die activities or decisions for the community, and who on the Board and staff should have responsibility for meeting those mission-related, do-or-die priorities.

In one evening, an overwhelming list of issues became a more manageable set of clear priorities for the Executive Director and the organization. The group also discussed ways of receiving community ideas that respected everyone's opinion but did not give the impression that all ideas would receive highest priority by the association.

It was decided that the community would be better informed through the existing newsletter regarding the mission, current priorities, and long-term goals of the association. The Board and the community-relations staff person also decided to hold a community forum twice a year to gather ideas and ask for input. Staff members were instructed to encourage community members to attend these forums to express their ideas and join Board committees that allowed non-Board members. Everyone agreed that if community members became more actively involved in finding solutions and taking ownership of their ideas, then the community would be better served.

In this neighborhood association the Executive Director struggled most with delegating to staff, to Board members as appropriate, and to community volunteers. Here is where the question of "Is this a leadership priority or a management priority?" becomes a valuable one to ask.

How can an Executive Director delegate when everyone is already busy?

We have found, in our work, that some Executive Directors think their staff or volunteers are already overburdened and should not be asked to take on any more work. At the same time, we have talked with staff who are looking for added responsibility and the opportunity to learn new skills. So if you feel you need help, ask—you may be doing people a favor rather than heaping burdens upon them. As you delegate new responsibilities, however, be sure to include some degree of added authority. When responsibilities are passed down without the required authority to get the job done, staff may become frustrated and may shrink away from further opportunities.

Other keys to success in delegation include clear communication and support. Don't simply adopt the "just do it" approach. Discussion should consider the purpose and importance of the task to be delegated in relationship to the employee's current priorities; understanding of the steps or process the task requires and a reasonable time-frame for completing it; and current priorities that the staff member can put aside until the delegated task is accomplished so as to keep the overall workload within reasonable bounds.

Some Executive Directors believe that delegating a task that was originally stated as a priority by the Board means shirking their own responsibilities. Not so, especially if the priority is a management issue. As a Board and Executive Director develop or renegotiate a work plan for the year, clear communication about tasks the Executive Director may wish to delegate to others is essential. Delegation of management issues allows opportunity for the Executive Director to maintain focus on the leadership priorities of the organization.

PART TWO

Executive Director as Visionary

You are not here merely to make a living. You are here in order to enable the world to live more amply, with greater vision, with a finer spirit of hope and achievement. You are here to enrich the world, and you impoverish yourself if you forget the errand.

—PRESIDENT WOODROW WILSON

AN EXECUTIVE DIRECTOR is often the person that Board and staff look to for inspiration and motivation. You, as the ED, have an invigorating passion for the cause you are serving, and you have a vision of greatness for your organization. It is this vision that holds people together and inspires them to come to work each day, raise necessary funds, provide governance and oversight, and serve the community well. Without vision, an organization may flounder, and struggle, and never attain greatness.

To create a powerful vision, the Executive Director must understand the culture of the nonprofit. What are the underlying values, beliefs, practices, and assumptions that guide the organization, and are deeply rooted? No vision can ever take hold that isn't built on the nonprofit's culture.

There is, however, more for an Executive Director to do than have a vision for the nonprofit. The vision must be shared by people inside and outside the organization, so it must be articulated, understood, massaged, and written down for all to see.

To achieve a vision, an organization must have a plan. Often this is a strategic plan that spans several years with goals and operational tasks that move the nonprofit ever closer to its vision.

Finally, for a vision to take hold and motivate everyone in the organization, people must believe that it is a fundamental element to the success of the nonprofit. The Executive Director and Board must be vigilant in defining what the word *success* means for their nonprofit in its efforts to achieve its vision, and must review progress toward this target regularly.

All these topics are covered in detail in this part of the book, starting first with understanding nonprofit culture in Chapter Four. Chapter Five defines *vision* and gives a road map for Executive Directors to create and articulate vision and plan for its achievement. Finally, Chapter Six provides practical advice on measuring organizational effectiveness toward the vision's attainment.

Understanding Nonprofit Organizational Culture

It seems right that cultures are formed from an unusual point of view, refined and strengthened by external and internal challenges, and led by a portfolio of people with complementary skills.

—Regina E. Herzlinger, "Culture Is the Key,"
Leading Beyond the Walls

Just as nations and societies have characteristic cultures, all groups, large or small, develop an identifiable culture of their own. Doing things the "HP way," the "Ben and Jerry's way," or the "Sun Microsystems way" are examples of corporate cultures. Government cultures are expressed in the behavior of council members, public agency officials and employees, and national leaders. Family cultures are often dominated by one or more parental value systems. Service organizations and clubs, such as the Kiwanis and your local soccer clubs, all have established norms and traditions that express their cultures.

Nonprofit organizations are no exception. Within each nonprofit is at least one dominant culture, and most have several subcultures. Culture is frequently unseen and unarticulated, yet it is always operating at the heart of any organization. When things are going smoothly, the culture is revered and honored. Conversely, an organization's culture can become the scapegoat for discontent or dissatisfaction, or for individuals or ideas that don't fit.

In this chapter we explore the meaning of nonprofit culture and how the effectiveness of an Executive Director depends upon understanding, defining, articulating, managing, and oftentimes changing this culture. As we explore nonprofit organizational culture, we will answer the following questions:

- What does *organizational culture* mean?
- How does understanding the organization's culture make the Executive Director more effective?
- How does an Executive Director determine what the organization's culture is?
- What are some strategies for changing or moving an organization's culture to where it needs to be in order to be successful?

What does *organizational culture* mean?

The term *organizational culture* emerged in the 1950s, followed by such terms as *organizational characteristics* and *organizational identity*. Here are two commonly applied definitions:

Edgar Schein: Organizational culture is the pattern of shared basic assumptions that the group learned as it solved its problems of external adaptation and internal integration, which has worked well enough to be considered valid and therefore to be taught to new members as the correct way to perceive, think, and feel in relation to those problems.

Roger Harrison and Herb Stokes: Organizational culture is the pattern of beliefs, values, rituals, myths, and sentiments shared by members of an organization.

For the purposes of this book, we are using the following definition, which emerges from the similarities and differences expressed in the definitions just noted.

> Organizational culture is made up of the often-unspoken assumption of values, beliefs, and processes that underlie the goals, work habits, decision making, conflict resolution, management, and perceived success of any organization. The culture includes the everyday patterns of work that have developed over time, and the deeper hidden assumptions and beliefs that consciously and unconsciously drive that work.

In most nonprofits, the initial identity was established by the Founder. It is this person's values, beliefs, and patterns of work that dominate the early days. As new people come into the organization and the Founder becomes less influential, one or several new cultures may emerge.

As organizations mature, their cultures develop or evolve through strong assumptions and values that Board members bring from their respective communities. For instance, influential Board members from corporations sometimes encourage a nonprofit to change its culture to one that is more like that found in business by inserting some of their own corporate assumptions and practices into the organization.

Having several cultures in a nonprofit can create a wonderful learning environment as people weave their values and beliefs together. Alternatively, a nonprofit with more than one culture can be thrown into chaos and major conflict as people try to dominate and impose their values and beliefs on others.

Organizations that are rich with a blend of values, assumptions, and personalities have wonderful opportunities to create a multi-culture that

Wisdom

Culture is the personality, the soul of the organization—respect it as a powerful force that can help or hinder your efforts to be successful. Find its strengths and utilize them well. Change the parts that no longer work.

is both positive and healthy. As an Executive Director of a multi-culture you have the important task of understanding as much as possible about the individual differences you are working with, and the responsibility to encourage everyone in the organization to develop a similar appreciation for the value of those differences.

Clients served by a nonprofit, as well as the broader community in which the organization operates, also contribute to organizational culture. Values, beliefs, and practices from those outside the organization often have an impact on staff and volunteers. For example, in nonprofits serving disenfranchised populations it is a practice to hire these individuals as paid and volunteer staff. They bring many of the values and beliefs they hold into the organization, and over time, these can translate into program priorities and new ways of working with clients that eventually become integrated into the organization's culture. Whether this interweaving of a client's culture into a nonprofit is an enhancement or a problem depends on the efforts of the Executive Director and all who work in the organization to recognize and understand the cultural characteristics.

How does understanding the organization's culture make the Executive Director more effective?

Almost everything you do as Executive Director is affected by the culture of the nonprofit where you work. The organizational vision, how people are or aren't recognized for good work, who makes what decisions, the communication patterns, how conflicts are or aren't resolved, what is rewarded, and how the organization responds to the larger community and client needs are all culturally based.

As Executive Director you have the option of reaffirming and building on the existing culture of your nonprofit or of changing a culture that has become dysfunctional and is not serving the organization or community well. To accomplish either of these objectives, particularly as an Executive Director new to the nonprofit, you must spend time understanding the culture of the organization you lead and how it has evolved from its founding to the present. You can then determine where the organization might need to go in the future.

The consequences of not taking time to understand the organizational culture can be serious. One classic example is the "bad fit phenomenon."

All too often Boards report that their Executive Director did not stay around very long: "It just wasn't a good fit," they say. We would suggest that a likely translation here is that the Executive Director didn't understand the organization's culture and tried to make changes in the nonprofit that ran into long-standing, deeply embedded norms and beliefs.

Generally, when this happens the Executive Director receives a cool reception to a new idea. When you hear "but that's not how we do things around here," you know that you have just bumped into a cultural barrier. You will probably discover that processes developed in the early days by the Founder worked well back then and now have become how people measure their success. Your idea threatens the security of the established culture. To move beyond this barrier requires patience and fortitude. Gaining allies within the organization through discussions of possible new ways to conduct the work is a necessary step because it creates buy-in with those individuals who will work with you to shift the culture.

That you understand the nature of your fit with an organization is essential. In fact, those Executive Directors who report being happy and enjoying their work, and who have established strong partnerships with others in the organization, are the ones who have found the fit for themselves. To understand if you and your organization fit well together, ask yourself these questions:

WARNING

Don't try to analyze an organization's culture alone. Engage your staff and even Board members in this exercise.

- Is my vision for this organization shared by the staff and Board?
- Are my values the same as the organization's?

- Are my ideas for changing practices and policies generally accepted rather than discarded?
- Do I have a positive relationship with people inside and outside the organization?
- Am I excited about my work most of the time, and committed to the mission?

If your answer is yes to these questions, then you probably have a good fit with your nonprofit.

In addition to the need for a good fit, understanding your organization's culture is important for a variety of reasons. It makes you more effective as a leader. It also allows you to build on the abilities of competent people around you and, on a bigger scale, it ensures that your organization is fulfilling its mission.

Understanding the culture also leads to a more sustainable vision. When deeply felt and commonly shared values guide the work of an organization and underlie the vision, this helps everyone stay focused on what is possible for clients and community. In short, understanding the nonprofit's culture enables your leadership efforts to create priorities for the future and establish a shared and exciting vision.

Story from the Field

One Executive Director, new to a mid-size regional nonprofit serving persons with disabilities, found she had staff members in her office every day complaining about other staff members and telling her to make things better. This was puzzling; the staff was full of bright and capable people, but they seemed to be completely unable to communicate with one another! It turned out that the culture as defined by the Founder—twenty-five years earlier— was one in which the Executive Director was expected to be "Mom" and take care of everyone in the organization. Even though several Executive Directors had come and gone since the Founder's time, the original culture was still dominant.

The new Executive Director had experienced similar norms in other organizations she had led, so she knew what to do. She went immediately to work on establishing a new culture that empowered staff to solve their own problems and work more closely with each other.

Her first step was to hold one-on-one meetings with her managers and tell them that she was most interested in their concerns and issues, but she expected them to bring her answers as well as problems. She also pointed out that if someone came to her to discuss another staff member, she wanted to hear about their attempts to get together to resolve their differences. The Executive Director said she was happy to be a coach to her managers so they could learn how to resolve conflicts themselves. She assured them that although they would probably make some mistakes along the way, she knew her managers could easily turn any mistakes into learning experiences.

Over time, managers became empowered to resolve their own problems and conflicts. The Executive Director, with her staff, started shifting the culture to a more positive one that encouraged staff to communicate with one another.

This story illustrates how one Executive Director used her understanding of her organization's culture to expand the capability of the staff to be more effective. In the process, she improved the general atmosphere and freed up her own time for other pressing obligations.

How does an Executive Director determine what the organization's culture is?

Regardless of how long you have been Executive Director of an organization, it's important to take some time to step back, take a deep breath, and attempt to define and articulate exactly what the culture is. First, realizing that no nonprofit has a culture exactly like any other, it is useful to understand what makes your nonprofit's culture unique and what it shares with others of similar background and outlook. Just as there may be similarities in the personalities of people, so too there may be similarities in the personalities of organizations, but regardless, each one is unique. A look at several key ingredients to organizational culture will help you to define yours.

The Founder's vision and beliefs: Nonprofits are typically started by someone who has found that a community or societal problem exists and is not being resolved. This Founder generally plays a major leadership role in the early days of the organization, often as a Board Chair or Executive Director. Usually the Founder has a very strong vision and beliefs about what should be changed in society, and these perceptions will dominate the organization's culture.

The articulated learnings of paid and unpaid staff: People working in a nonprofit usually learn how to get something done from someone who has done the job before. Even when the organization has written policies or procedures, job tasks are most often just passed verbally along from one person to another. Learning originates from how people observe, assess, and implement any given task.

The common processes that remain in effect over time: Less apparent are communication and decision-making processes developed by a nonprofit's Founder and the first Board of Directors that may remain in effect years later. Who hears what information and who is involved in which decisions is often determined by the initially established processes for moving information through the organization to the designated people the original leadership group believed must have it.

The unspoken assumptions that have built up over time: Unspoken assumptions usually guide the behavior of staff and volunteers in the organization, telling them how to think and feel about working there. Such assumptions can be found underlying all aspects of the culture, and are usually not articulated. For example, staff may share the assumption that the Board of Directors is not in tune with the organization. This

Wisdom

Remember that many deep-rooted conflicts in organizations are caused by differing cultures. Sometimes it is important to look beyond the immediate surface-level problem to consider the underlying assumptions or other aspects of culture that may be contributing to conflict. Work from there to find resolution.

makes it difficult for Board members to build trust and credibility with staff, and puts the Executive Director into an awkward position of taking sides. The assumptions may have been established years ago and have nothing to do with the current members of the Board.

The values that shape and guide the organization's purpose: In a nonprofit, the values are likely to be deeply felt and altruistic. The people working in the organization will be passionate about these values whether they are spoken or not. Values will differ greatly from nonprofit to nonprofit. Staff in your organization may share the value of honoring differences in culture, or preserving open space for future generations, or ensuring dignity and choice for frail elders. These values appear in the mission statement and are part of all programs and services in the organization.

Some nonprofits seem to have no prevailing culture. This is seen in organizations where there is rapid turnover, especially in the leadership. It becomes difficult to build a shared experience and to articulate common learnings. Policies and procedures change depending on who has the loudest voice at the moment, and conflict is often pervasive because communication processes have broken down. The apparent absence of organizational culture usually indicates that several cultures are vying to be the strongest.

WARNING

Don't ever underestimate the power of the nonprofit culture!

Exhibit 4.1 provides a list of questions to ask paid and unpaid staff and Board members to help define an organization's culture. When you have fully explored the answers, you can summarize the findings into a clear definition of your nonprofit's culture. This can then be shared with everyone currently in the nonprofit and anyone new who joins the organization.

We recommend you take a few months to answer all these questions with staff and Board members, or do so in a day-long retreat setting. These are questions that will trigger a lot of thought and discussion. It may be desirable to bring in an outside facilitator to work with everyone, so you are free to offer your opinions as a member of the group.

As staff and volunteers participate in answering these questions, be watchful for responses that differ and may conflict with one another.

Exhibit 4.1 Understanding an Organization's Culture

Vision, Values, and Beliefs

- What are the inherent values that emanate from our mission and drive our day-to-day work?

- What, if any, are the conflicting values held by people working here?

- What values inspire our vision and make us unique?

Learnings

- How do staff and volunteers learn how to do their jobs?

- If people make a mistake in this organization, how are they treated?

- What motivates people to get their work done?

- What behavior is rewarded and what is not?

- How is performance success measured?

Processes

- What are our values and beliefs regarding who makes what decisions? Do these help or hinder effective decision-making processes?

- Is internal communication friendly and supportive, nonexistent, or competitive? Why?

- What are our values regarding conflict resolution? Does our culture help or hinder successful conflict resolution?

Assumptions

- What is expected of the people who work here as staff members, volunteers, or Board members?

- Does our culture assume each person is a member of the family, or someone hired to get the job done, or something else?

- What assumptions do we make about our clients? How do these assumptions affect our work with them?

Wrap-Up Question

- What do we like about ourselves as an organization? What values, assumptions, processes, and learnings present barriers for us?

Grouping responses at the end of a discussion can be helpful in discovering patterns that articulate different cultures. For instance, an all-volunteer animal rescue organization was deeply enmeshed in inexplicable conflict. After answering some of the questions in Exhibit 4.1, they grouped their responses and discovered two dominant cultures—one that felt the nonprofit needed to be more business oriented, and the other that felt that rescuing animals rose above everything else—including spending funds wisely. Clarifying these two distinct cultures helped the organization resolve some of its conflicts and move forward.

Several tools and instruments for evaluating culture also exist on the market. These are noted in the Resources section for this chapter. While each of these tools has some value, a note of caution is needed because they all provide a set of criteria to enable you to neatly classify your organization with a specific label. In other words, if you answer the questions this way, then you are a certain type of nonprofit. Neither human personalities nor organizational personalities can be so easily categorized.

What are some strategies for changing or moving an organization's culture to where it needs to be in order to be successful?

Changing an organization's culture is no small task; it needs to be done attentively and gradually, allowing sufficient time for adaptation and integration. The following exercise is one way to shift the culture.

1. Acknowledge and put language around what is and isn't working well in your nonprofit by working through the questions in Exhibit 4.1.
2. Revisit the same set of questions in the exhibit, but this time have everyone answer them in terms of what they personally want or prefer for the organization, rather than what currently is.
3. Compare the two sets of answers.

If the first and second sets of responses are similar—in other words, people seem relatively satisfied—and if the organization is meeting community needs well, then it may not be time to make any major cultural shifts. Rather, you should articulate and celebrate your culture. On the other hand, if you notice significant differences between the two sets of responses, then you know that you need to gently introduce a process that will change some or all aspects of the culture that are dysfunctional.

One way to introduce this process is to meet with the Board Executive Committee and describe the differences you found in the responses to the questions. Explain why these differences are creating some dysfunction in the organization and why you feel a change is needed. Have the committee discuss why they think these differences exist and what might be done about them. Get the committee's buy-in for making changes in the culture.

When you have the committee's buy-in, have the same conversation with your management team or key staff and volunteers to help them understand the situation and get their support. You also might brainstorm with both the Executive Committee and key staff about what a healthier culture for the nonprofit could look like.

After you have the all-important agreement of your Executive Committee and key staff, you can clearly articulate changes you would like to make to shift the culture from dysfunction to health. In the case of the animal rescue organization mentioned earlier, the Board President (also serving as the Executive Director) held a meeting with all interested volunteers during which he described the significant cultural conflict of some volunteers wanting to run an efficient business model and others wanting to rescue all animals regardless of cost. He asked for individuals to help him shift the culture to one where the nonprofit could operate efficiently and still rescue those animals most in need. After several months of hard work, there was a noticeable shift in the culture as the conflict and tension in the organization was significantly reduced.

CHAPTER FIVE

Creating and Sustaining a Vision

*Unimpeded on a daily basis by the concern for survival, free from
the generalized assumption of scarcity, a person [that is, a visionary]
stands in the great place of possibility in a posture of openness, with
an unfettered imagination for what can be.*
— ROSAMUND AND BENJAMIN ZANDER, *The Art of Possibility*

BEING A VISIONARY requires someone to have imagination and to dream
about what is possible. Martin Luther King Jr. was one of this society's
greatest visionaries. His "I have a dream" speech was his vision; it has
inspired greatness in generations of people committed to social change.

Executive Directors are often the visionaries for their organizations.
Sometimes it is a Board member and sometimes it is a key stakeholder
whose vision inspires the beginnings of the nonprofit—but mostly it is the
Executive Director who imagines what is possible and dares to make it so.

This chapter addresses the concept of vision by way of the following questions:

- What is a vision and why is it important?
- What are ways for an Executive Director to articulate and develop
  a shared organizational vision?

- Why is planning important to the vision process in a nonprofit, and what is the Executive Director's role in this process?
- If you're always in crisis or catch-up mode as an Executive Director, how do you find time to plan?

What is a vision and why is it important?

In *The Leadership Challenge* James Kouzes and Barry Posner define the word *vision* as "an ideal and unique image of the future." That is, a vision is your picture of what is possible for your organization. It evolves into a shared dream for your organization.

Visions are never negative! They always picture hope and greatness, and aim at changing the world for those you serve. Kouzes and Posner give the following characteristics for vision:

- Vision suggests future orientation.
- Vision connotes a standard of excellence, an ideal. It implies a choice of values.
- Vision has the quality of uniqueness. It hints at what makes something special.

It is about the future, about organizational excellence, and it's about your nonprofit's uniqueness. Vision is important for the organization because, without it, no one in the organization—including the Executive Director—ever feels inspired to move beyond the daily grind and create new opportunities for fulfilling the nonprofit's mission.

Often, the lack of vision can mean a lack of focus for the organization as well. The famous saying "if you don't know where you are going, then anywhere will do" speaks to this lack of focus and direction. When there is vision, there is focus, which in turn helps the nonprofit expend

Wisdom

Having a vision for your organization gives everyone involved a sense of excitement about the future as well as focus and direction.

resources wisely and channel the energy of staff, volunteers, and Board members in a single direction toward the future.

What are ways for an Executive Director to articulate and develop a shared organizational vision?

Developing your own vision for the organization may be the easy step in building an organizational vision with the commitment for achieving it. Your vision for the organization comes from your own experience as well as from assumptions you have about the organization and the community you serve. Mostly though, the vision you have will come from your heart—from what you feel is possible. It is not just an intellectual exercise, although some intellect is involved. Your vision is also based on your gut instinct.

Having your own vision for the organization isn't enough, though. For your vision to become reality, it must be built and shared by paid and unpaid staff, Board members, and external stakeholders. This is crucial because an effective vision must live beyond its first proponent's time in the organization. Thus your own vision for your nonprofit is only the starting point; it is the base for the one that is shared.

Wisdom

Your vision for your nonprofit comes from your gut instincts as well as your experience, knowledge, and mental picture of the current situation. Of all the elements that go into creating your vision, trusting your instincts may be the most valuable.

To create a shared vision, you may want to check out some of your assumptions and instincts with members of your Board and staff so you have some initial input into it. As you think through your vision, share it with everyone, listen to their feedback, and try on their ideas for the future. Build a true organizational vision with the added imagination and wisdom of everyone.

There are many ways to include internal stakeholders in a visioning process. Internally, you might schedule a "vision retreat" where Board, staff, and key volunteers come together to discuss, modify, and ultimately embrace what must become their vision. This is an opportunity to build excitement and inspire people to believe in a great new future.

Externally, you can share the vision of the organization with key stakeholders at an event, or a public meeting, or as part of an interview published in the local paper. Our belief is that the more people who know the organization's vision and support it, the better it is for the nonprofit. A shared vision is an opportunity to attract donors and gain important allies or stakeholders for your mission.

Story from the Field

Here is what happened to one busy Executive Director who didn't take the time to share her vision. This ED came to a performing arts organization in the footsteps of someone who had served as Executive Director for twelve years. Staff and Board members had been there almost as long. The organization had been stable for most of those years with a steady stream of funding and popular performances. Recently though, long-standing funders had moved on to newer, more innovative arts groups, and audiences were falling off.

One of the first things the new Executive Director realized was that the vision of the previous ED was no longer big, bold, and exciting to everyone. The organization was in the doldrums, new performing artists were not being pursued, and morale was low.

The Executive Director was excited about the possibilities for the organization. She spent several months thinking and talking about—and testing assumptions about—what direction the nonprofit could move in that would create excitement and expand artistic awareness in the community. Eventually she wrote down her vision, and shared it with Mim. It was powerful, ambitious, and full of energy and inspiration. Mim encouraged her to share it with her Board and staff to build on it, and create a shared excitement.

Before she had a chance to share the vision further, however, a series of small crises hit the organization. Some staff left, leaving important positions to be filled. The largest funder decided it had given this arts group enough money, and one performing season was roundly criticized in the press. The vision got lost in the day-to-day struggles of the organization.

WARNING

Imagining the possibilities for your organization all by yourself and setting forth the vision is a recipe for disaster. The organization's vision should be developed and shared by all key stakeholders.

After one year of working at this organization, the Executive Director still had not shared her vision with staff and Board. The group held an organizational retreat for all Board and staff members, and at this day-long planning meeting, many conflicts arose over direction and focus of the organization. The Executive Director became frustrated at one point, and blurted out, "What you want for this organization is not part of my vision!" In great surprise, everyone asked her what her vision was, and she shared it. Happily, Board and staff loved it and began talking about how to achieve it. Once the vision was shared, planning turned into an easy task for the organization.

This story illustrates that when Executive Directors forget to share their visions, conflicts can pull their staff and Board members in many directions. When a vision is shared, the nonprofit can get focused and move forward at great speed.

Why is planning important to the vision process in a nonprofit, and what is the Executive Director's role in this process?

Once the organization has a strong and exciting vision, it's usually necessary to have a plan that gives the specifics on how to achieve it. Creating the vision becomes the first step to planning.

Planning occurs at several levels in a nonprofit:

- Organization-wide strategic plans
- Annual program and operating plans
- Fund development plans
- Individual work plans

The most successful nonprofits tie all their annual planning activities to the strategic plan. To measure the organization's success, these plans are monitored with periodic evaluations designed to provide good information on levels of effectiveness and areas that may need redirected efforts.

In organizations with paid staff, planning is primarily a staff-driven activity, especially at the program and operations level. Board members are expected to engage in strategic planning at the macro level, providing input to the mission statement, vision, and values. Depending on their knowledge of the organization and its programs, the Board members may also provide guidance in setting priorities. Of course, in organizations without staff, Board members are the planners as well as the doers.

The Executive Director is generally the person who sets the tone for planning and leads the various processes in the organization. For instance, an Executive Director who sees the value of planning will exercise leadership to move the organization to have planning processes at work. They will become part of the culture of the organization. On the other hand, if the Executive Director is averse to planning, this resistance will effectively keep the nonprofit from engaging in these important processes.

An Executive Director does not have to do all the planning, but must make sure that everyone understands the value of it. Without the Executive Director's leadership, planning is likely to not happen.

Warning

Don't try to do all the planning yourself; no matter how good you are, the results won't be as strong or as well-supported as they would be if the people who will carry out the plan were involved in making it.

If you're always in crisis or catch-up mode as an Executive Director, how do you find time to plan?

The first thing to do is step back and understand what is causing the feelings of crisis or catch-up. Is this a temporary status for the organization, for instance a funding cut that demands immediate attention? Or is this an ongoing chronic condition? Sometimes there really is some immediate priority that must be addressed before engaging in planning, but more often the perception that there is no time to plan means that the organization is in an almost constant crisis mode.

In reality, the absence of planning is often what causes the crisis or apparent need to catch up. When feelings of panic or stress kick in during difficult times, it is hard to imagine sitting down to come up with a plan. Yet this may well be the most essential step to moving beyond the current situation. Taking a few hours to do some short-term planning can save an Executive Director countless hours of stress and worry down the road.

Also, remember that the Executive Director does not have to do all the planning personally. As the leader, the ED is expected to provide vision for the organization and to make sure planning happens. In very small organizations where the Executive Director is the whole staff, the Board of Directors should be heavily engaged in mission and vision discussions, in setting direction and priorities, and determining their own role in achieving them. In larger organizations, the staff and volunteers are there to actively participate in setting annual goals and implementation strategies. They also are essential to getting the goals met for the year.

When an Executive Director views the organization in crisis, ongoing planning processes may need to be temporarily suspended while crisis planning takes the forefront. But ongoing planning processes should not be forgotten. If the perception is that the nonprofit is always catching up, then the plans that have been set may be too ambitious. The Executive Director's leadership is needed to communicate with everyone in the organization that planning is needed to reset priorities and make work more doable. Plans are not set in stone, and the Executive Director's leadership helps allow for the flexibility needed to ensure the organization is moving forward at a realistic pace.

Planning is essential to achieving your vision. If Board, staff, and volunteers have a blueprint for moving the organization toward the vision, then everyone will know what is important for them to accomplish.

CHAPTER SIX

Determining Organizational Effectiveness

Each mission must be thought through in terms of results. People are no longer simply interested to know, is it a good cause? Instead they want to see a demonstration of achievement as a responsible and effective organization.

—PETER DRUCKER, Leader to Leader Institute

WHEN A NONPROFIT is seen as serving its community effectively, it's a fair guess to say a remarkable Executive Director is leading this organization.

Determining nonprofit effectiveness goes beyond good intentions, numbers of people served, or the financial bottom line. It is more than evaluating a single program or set of activities, achievements, or outcomes. It is measured in terms of achieving the overall goals in the organization's strategic plan and fulfilling the organization's mission.

This chapter looks at ways Executive Directors can encourage and evaluate the effectiveness of an organization, and how that success ties to their own. It addresses these questions:

- What does an effective nonprofit organization look like?
- How soon after starting should the Executive Director begin to examine the organization's effectiveness?

- How does an Executive Director tie personal performance and effectiveness to that of the organization?
- What happens if the Board and Executive Director determine the organization is no longer effective?

What does an effective nonprofit organization look like?

The question of recognizing effectiveness goes to the heart of this book. The simple answer is that an effective organization is one that can demonstrate results toward achieving its mission. The answer assumes that the mission is still relevant and the results are measurable. It also assumes that the organizational culture values feedback, continuous leaning, and improvement. That is where simplicity ends and the complex job of defining an effective nonprofit organization begins. There are dozens of tools, methods, and types of evaluations that nonprofits can employ to help evaluate organizational effectiveness. We have assembled a list of resources for the chapter at the end of the book to guide and inform your process. Exhibit 6.1 summarizes some of the more common methods.

By using the methods listed in the exhibit, an organization can conduct needs assessments to make sure its mission and programs are still relevant, determine new trends in or affecting the nonprofit, monitor organizational effectiveness, and conduct feasibility studies for possible new programs or partnerships.

Many EDs believe that proving their organizations' effectiveness requires highly complex processes, almost always involving the employment of outside experts at a significant expense. Others are sure they simply know what's best and define effectiveness based upon personal perceptions. The reality is that the processes for measuring and defining organizational effectiveness range from highly personal and overly

Wisdom

Evaluation need not be costly or time-consuming. It can start by simply asking what is working and what is not.

Exhibit 6.1 Methods of Gathering Feedback on Effectiveness

Here is a sample of the most common methods nonprofits use to determine effectiveness by capturing reactions, feelings, learnings, or changes in anything from objective numbers to subjective attitudes. Each method's application will vary depending on the focus or depth of the evaluation, the audience, the information to be assessed, and the time line or budget.

- Interviews

- Focus groups

- Surveys

- Audits

- Questionnaires

- Observation

- Documentation or literature review

- Case studies

simplistic to extremely complex and theoretical assessments where the outcome can be lost in the process. Evaluating effectiveness doesn't need to be complex, costly, or externally managed. But it does require an organization-wide culture that openly embraces the following characteristics in both the organization and the Executive Director:

- Awareness of the emerging trends that affect the organization, your mission, and your clients, coupled with the agility to create responsive programs and systems.
- Insightfulness to look deep into the nonprofit's underlying culture and articulate it, along with the strength to change it if necessary.
- Ability to form and nurture positive relationships with Board members, paid and unpaid staff, and external stakeholders that allow the organization to pursue mutually agreed-upon goals effectively.

- Initiative to explore and form partnerships and strategic alliances that build on shared strengths to develop the nonprofit's capacity to serve its community.

- Vision for the organization and an ability to articulate it in a way that inspires others.

- Resourcefulness to attract adequate resources of time, talent, and funding to keep the organization thriving, and to ensure they are wisely invested.

- Openness to feedback and an environment of continuous learning that monitors individual and organizational effectiveness.

- Courage to improve upon or change what isn't working well.

Every nonprofit displays these characteristics differently, but they are an essential foundation for an effective organization to build programs and services. Without this foundation, the best evaluation processes and tools will encounter resistance or inaction.

How soon after starting should the Executive Director begin to examine the organization's effectiveness?

The short answer to the question of timing is, right away! An Executive Director new to the organization needs to understand the current environment—what is working and what is not, what is in place and what isn't. Many nonprofits will undertake an assessment process or audit as a prelude to their search process to help them define the skills and experience they need in their new ED. If this hasn't been done, newly hired Executive Directors need to initiate a review process of finances, management, programs, systems, the Board, community relations, fundraising, and staff within the first few weeks. The information gathered will help drive the ED's priorities and negotiate performance expectations with the Board.

WARNING

Without a culture that embraces learning and continuous improvement, the best evaluation processes and tools encounter resistance or inaction.

To begin conversations with staff and volunteers, Board members, and occasionally key external stakeholders about the effectiveness of the organization, we suggest asking each person these five simple but insightful sets of questions:

- What do you think this organization is very good at doing? What have been its greatest accomplishments?

- What are barriers facing the organization? Facing the Board? Facing the staff or volunteers?

- Of those barriers, which ones are the highest priority to address?

- What is it we are trying to accomplish with our programs? How do we measure if we are successful?

- If this organization were operating at its peak, what would that look like? What would the organization be doing differently?

Gathering this information from internal as well as external sources gives an Executive Director a broadly interpreted picture of the organization's strengths and the challenges it faces and helps define and prioritize the issues to resolve. The information also gives the ED an understanding of what individuals think the organization is successful at doing, what it needs to do better, and what success would look like if the organization were functioning at its optimum.

Wisdom

The Executive Director's job is to lead the evaluation process, not fix all the problems.

Sometimes newly hired Executive Directors are so eager to please that they make promises during these initial conversations that simply can't be kept. Feelings of being overwhelmed and stretched too far often result from unrealistic promises or expectations set in the first few months on the job. A better approach is to make it clear that the purpose of the conversation is to gather information about the current state of the organization, meet everyone, and establish jointly developed priorities for the future.

Another common thought held by Executive Directors is that once all the information is gathered and a good picture of the organization has emerged, then it becomes the ED's job to do it all—to personally provide everything the organization needs. That's a noble intention, but generally impossible to fulfill.

A better practice is to make sure that key internal stakeholders in the organization (typically the Board and management staff) agree with your insights and your solutions. It is a shared responsibility of Board and staff to work with the Executive Director to break down any barriers and set realistic next steps.

The Executive Director's job is to lead the process, not just fix the problems. The ED can lead the process by

- Identifying strengths and challenges and communicating them to the staff and Board of Directors.
- Building a new vision of success that energizes and inspires everyone in the organization.
- Seeking solutions and motivating others to carry them out.

How does an Executive Director tie personal performance and effectiveness to that of the organization?

Just as organizations need some level of self-assessment to evaluate their effectiveness, Executive Directors need feedback from their organizations on their own effectiveness. The first challenge is making time for the process. The second challenge is determining appropriate indicators that adequately tie the effectiveness of the individual to that of the nonprofit.

Even though the hiring and evaluation of the Executive Director is one of the few specific governance roles spelled out as part of a nonprofit's incorporation papers, many Boards are delinquent in these duties, leaving the Executive Director in the awkward role of requesting feedback and designing the process. Rather than postpone the

WARNING

EDs need to engage their Boards in a process to jointly identify and prioritize key indicators by which their performance will be measured.

discussion to a formal annual event, invite casual ongoing feedback and opportunities to discuss mid-course corrections. Newer EDs will often ask the Board Chair or Executive Committee for verbal feedback after the first three or six months. Seasoned EDs who find themselves caught up in a challenge or crisis often seek feedback on how they are doing and ways that they might improve or learn from any mistakes.

WARNING

Don't leave ED evaluation to the whim of the Board.

The second challenge is in developing appropriate indicators or measurements. Without specific goals or indicators, some evaluations turn into popularity contests, asking generic questions that capture individual perceptions but seldom get to the heart of the ED's effectiveness at leading the organization or accomplishments against specific goals. Useful indicators may be narrow or broad, but they need to be defined for the specific priorities of the organization.

For instance, say your organization serves homeless children and families. A Board indicator of success could be the number of families who left the streets and moved into their own apartments by a specific date. While the Executive Director may not be directly involved in getting individual families off the streets, the leadership the ED provides the organization is responsible for its success in this area.

Another key indicator of success is the tenure and effectiveness of staff, volunteers, and Board members. If the average tenure is long, then this probably means that the work environment empowers people to do their best. Again, it is the Executive Director's leadership that is responsible. If the Executive Director does not build and maintain good working relationships with everyone inside the organization, and is not motivating, inspiring, and encouraging each person to learn and grow on the job, then the organization is not being as successful as it could be.

For many Executive Directors, the indicators will already be established as part of a strategic plan and of the annual work plans for staff. For EDs leading a local affiliate of a national or regional organization, indicators may be mandated by charter.

The task of defining and prioritizing five to ten indicators that realistically define effectiveness for the organization can lead to a healthy discussion between the Executive Director, the Board, and staff. When the indicators are agreed upon, then they become the foundation of the ED evaluation process.

But what do you do if the organization has no strategic plan, no national mandate, no work plans? Perhaps the nonprofit is in formation, or just emerged from a transition with plans not yet in place, or people have not made planning a priority. You don't need to hold off until a comprehensive strategic plan is in place to decide what makes your organization successful and measures the ED's performance. Exhibit 6.2 outlines a process you can use if no indicators have been developed yet. You may also find it useful to refer to Chapter Ten, where we discuss developing a work plan with your Board.

The creation of criteria that measure effectiveness in the nonprofit and in ED performance may also be a first step to beginning the longer-term planning process that has eluded the organization.

Exhibit 6.2 Defining Performance Measures

As Executive Director, you will probably have to identify some, if not all, of the indicators that measure the organization's short-term success and can be tied to your own performance. Working in partnership with your full Board or a smaller committee, you can do the following:

1. Identify the critical issues or barriers facing the organization based upon some process of assessment or reflection.

2. Determine three to five priorities that are critical to addressing these issues or barriers, or to achieving the organization's vision or achieving organizational effectiveness.

3. Incorporate the priorities into the annual ED evaluation process and make sure they are communicated to and adopted by the Board and staff.

4. Establish opportunities for regular feedback to the ED and a process for renegotiating these factors as necessary in response to internal or external shifts.

What happens if the Board and Executive Director determine the organization is no longer effective?

This question starts from the assumption that the Board and Executive Director have identified what effectiveness looks like for their nonprofit. They may have used the characteristics listed earlier in this chapter and discovered few similarities to their organization. Or there may be external criteria unique to that organization that are no longer being met, which could result in a loss of funding, regulatory approval, or community confidence. Whatever the reasons, this is a time for some long soul-searching discussions.

The truth is that some nonprofits become obsolete because their programs have been so successful that the problem has been eradicated, as with polio in the United States. Others lose touch with shifting trends and community priorities, or with their clients' needs. They may suffer a major loss of talent or resources, or experience monumental internal struggles that make it impossible to maintain effectiveness.

Everyone in the organization needs to be creative about the future. It is important for the Executive Director to be fair-minded and encourage these other ideas to be stated and incorporated into decisions being made about the nonprofit. Remember that an Executive Director does not have to be the only leader in the organization. Others will step forward, especially when tough decisions are being made, and the Executive Director needs to stay open to possibilities that may seem startling or even unimaginable at first glance.

Restructuring or closing a nonprofit organization is often emotional for those involved. You are not alone. Every year, nonprofit organizations cease operations. Usually, nonprofits consider three main options: merger, closing down, and strategic reorganization. Within these options are an infinite number of possibilities depending on the vision and creativity of the organization. (See Chapter Nine on leading organizational

Wisdom

A complete loss of effectiveness is generally due to several factors and happens over several years. Rather than attempting the impossible task of deciding who is responsible, focus on some of the trends internal and external to the organization that have contributed to the loss.

change and Chapter Fourteen on partnerships and mergers for more help in making this difficult decision.)

When an organization is no longer effective, the Executive Director needs to be a very strong leader. People in the organization tend to blame or find fault when the nonprofit is struggling; they often point the finger directly but wrongly at the ED. Change can be difficult, but organizational restructuring or closure is traumatic, especially if it is seen only in negative terms.

The ED's parting leadership challenge is to create a positive ending and acknowledge past accomplishments as well as challenges. Organizations whose people can buy into the decision (no matter how difficult), speak with one voice, and move forward are recognized for finding solutions that can best meet client needs and fulfill their mission. Keeping focused on the mission and what is best for those served is of paramount importance in creating a positive ending.

PART THREE

Executive Director as Change Agent

They always say time changes things, but you actually have to change them yourself.

—ANDY WARHOL, *The Philosophy of Andy Warhol*

NONPROFIT ORGANIZATIONS are facing an extraordinary time of change as consumer needs become more complex, technology alters the way we communicate, funders increase their demands for accountability and measurable outcomes, and organizations recognize the need to monitor the evolving marketplace. Staying ahead of the curve becomes critical as Executive Directors try to keep their organizations strong and relevant.

While viewing the evolving world outside the nonprofit, Executive Directors must look internally also. Nonprofits move through a life cycle that represents numerous changes for the organization, requiring the ED to understand and provide leadership during this internal evolution.

Leading internal change doesn't always come easily. Many healthy nonprofits have foundered as their Executive Directors tried valiantly to help them embrace the need to change to meet a crisis or seize an opportunity. Staff is understandably resistant to change that may affect their personal turf. Boards can be skeptical of the benefits of new ways of doing things, and the consumers may only be able to focus on the short-term impact on themselves instead of the long-term benefits to the community.

Chapter Seven explores the changing nonprofit sector and new trends that are emerging in the twenty-first century. We also focus attention inward, in Chapter Eight, explaining organizational life cycles and how Executive Directors need to grow and change along with their nonprofits. Finally, we talk specifically about ways to manage change and lead a healthy change process in Chapter Nine.

By looking both externally and internally, an Executive Director can be a successful change agent in the organization. At the heart of all this change lies the mission of the nonprofit and the need to ensure a healthy and stable organization that can continue to fulfill its mission.

Embracing a Changing Nonprofit Environment

Contrary to the common belief that the nonprofit sector should operate more like a business, we should instead be remodeling business to look more like nonprofits.

—PAUL LIGHT, New York University

THE NONPROFIT SECTOR is one of the most exciting, complex, and rapidly changing sectors of the modern economy. As an Executive Director, you are faced on all sides with incredible opportunities, shifting revenue sources, changing societal needs, evolving government and business values, emerging competition, and ever-increasing public scrutiny. The next decade will challenge you and the entire sector to respond with new thinking, new systems, expanded capacity to learn and adapt, greater resilience, and an increased capacity to integrate change into every aspect of your organization.

By your very purpose, you, as Executive Director, are a champion of change in your community.

As you embrace the opportunities of this fast-moving sector it can be useful to consider the following thought-provoking questions about how the sector is evolving:

- Why is change synonymous with the identity of the nonprofit sector?

- How are the lines that have traditionally defined the business and nonprofit sectors changing?

- What are the new demands for accountability and measurable outcomes?

Why is change synonymous with the identity of the nonprofit sector?

Over time, the term *nonprofit* has been defined in myriad ways, from "a reflection of the collective consciousness of society" to "a legal tax advantage in exchange for doing good." In addition, the sector has been branded with a broad range of labels, most of which have clouded rather than clarified an understanding of exactly what a nonprofit is. Labels such as *NGOs (nongovernmental organizations), social entrepreneurs, public benefit corporations,* or *the Third Sector* have painted a better picture of what it is not than of what it is. Attempts to define, classify, and explain the sector in theoretical and economic terms have also failed to establish agreement on a definition.

One definition, however, has survived the test of time; it seems as valid today in the twenty-first century as it was throughout the twentieth century. Nonprofit organizations are consistently seen as the conduit through which individuals channel their ideals, passions, and resources and initiate change that is intended to improve the lives of the people they serve and the communities in which they live.

In contrast to the mission of business to generate profits, or that of government to control and administer, the mission of the nonprofit sector is to create a better world. Thus, the identity of nonprofits is all about making change happen.

Wisdom

Be vigilant of the rapidly changing issues in the nonprofit sector so that your organization can respond with new ways of thinking that will keep it strong and relevant.

The nonprofit sector has served as an incubator for some of the most significant social, ecological, political, and technological ideas of the past century. From neighborhood development to term limits for elected officials, from child care to higher education, nonprofits continue to touch nearly every facet of life. To continue implementing constructive change and transform communities, the nonprofit sector must maintain its own internal vigilance as to what changes it needs to make, including how its own identity affects how it is perceived and what it can ultimately accomplish. The simple choice of referring to your organization as a nongovernmental or nonprofit organization rather than a public benefit corporation or the social enterprise partner of XYZ Corporation may further define your organization's culture, values, and responsiveness to change.

Through strong leadership, the ED can help an organization translate shifts and changes in the sector into innovative opportunities to achieve its mission.

How are the lines that have traditionally defined the business and nonprofit sectors changing?

Growth of the nonprofit sector and its shifting revenues have resulted in a new and very different operating environment. As nonprofit organizations are being challenged to be more businesslike and accountable, business sector values are shifting toward a nonprofit-like, inclusive environment with greater engagement of stakeholders and collaborative strategic alliances. For example, a significant factor in Ben and Jerry's highly acclaimed brand of ice cream is the company's ability to tie social activism to the marketing of products such as "Peace Pops" and "One Sweet Whirled."

Nonprofits have historically taken on services and causes considered to be unprofitable by business or politically risky by government. In exchange, they have relied upon government and corporate support to fund their work. Corporations donate and invest in nonprofits to promote the development of responsive programs to help strengthen the communities in which their employees and stakeholders live.

WARNING

Don't let traditional boundaries or definitions of the nonprofit sector keep you from exploring innovative partnerships and business models.

However, businesses and nonprofits are aligning in new ways to reach beyond traditional support. As nonprofit organizations work to diversify and strengthen their funding streams, they are embracing new business opportunities that blend philanthropy and venture funding into *venture philanthropy* relationships with long-term investors. Other nonprofits are adopting entrepreneurial programs that generate earned income to support their missions and often position these programs to compete with business.

For example, technology-inspired organizations such as CompuMentor, TechSoup, and DiscounTech took a new approach to making technology product donations more available to nonprofits. Their approach enables corporations such as Microsoft, Cisco, and AOL to support the sector more effectively. Through their collaboration with leading technology providers, they combine easy access and discounted products with much-needed support that benefits both the nonprofit and private sectors.

Many nonprofits are able to successfully maneuver these blurring sector lines. Others find it difficult to be financially successful and still remain true to their mission. The challenge to nonprofit leadership is to balance faithfulness to the mission with a sustainable business model for funding the organization. In all your management practices, you must work hard to maintain room for the cause while you keep your eyes on the change you are trying to implement in your community.

What are the new demands for accountability and measurable outcomes?

The demand for accountability is not just a derivative of bull and bear markets on Wall Street, nor simply an outcome of the political scandals that enmesh elected government leaders. Nonprofit organizations, in exchange for their tax-exempt status, are charged with the legal responsibility to uphold the public trust.

Once upon a time, nonprofits upheld the public trust by first doing good work and then telling heartfelt stories of client transformation to verify their organization's effectiveness in meeting needs. Public and private donor scrutiny has moved the focus of measuring success to documentation of numbers and types of initiatives or services. The focus has further shifted in the past few years toward balancing overall fiscal accountability with individual program effectiveness. Nonprofits are now often asked to objectively demonstrate how each program or activity undertaken measurably affects the client, the core problem, and the needs, values, or causes that define the mission. A balanced budget and reasonable operating reserve level are no longer sufficient as measures of an effective organization.

The diversification of the nonprofit sector has led to the increased involvement of a greater variety of stakeholders. As a result, communication of your accomplishments must be in terms and language that resonate with your specific populations of stakeholders. Some will measure your success in terms of the fulfillment of your promise to their community. Others may want you to define your outcomes in terms of return on investment.

WARNING

Organizations that fail to embrace new ideas and change risk becoming ineffective and irrelevant.

While nonprofits have long been perceived as holding themselves to a higher standard of conduct than organizations in the corporate or government environments, the sector has unfortunately been rocked by its own scandals and misguided efforts. As a nonprofit leader, you must constantly encourage yourself, your organization, and your Board to embrace your collective due diligence roles. You cannot hesitate to ask the obvious and often difficult questions.

With the many internal and external priorities that Executive Directors face, it is sometimes easy to set aside the need for reviewing the trends that are changing the nonprofit sector. Executive Directors need to be vigilant of issues and trends in order to keep their organizations responsive, innovative, and resilient.

CHAPTER EIGHT

Understanding Changing Life Cycle Stages in Nonprofits

In addition to adapting to external factors such as funding cutbacks, organizations must also make periodic adjustments in response to their own internal evolution.
—Nancy Franco, Susan Gross, and Karl Mathiasen III,
The Management Assistance Group

Nonprofit organizations evolve just as the whole nonprofit sector does. In addition to being responsive to the changing external environment, Executive Directors must watch for the internal changes in their nonprofits that are natural to its life cycle. Most nonprofits move through life cycles much as human beings do; it can be useful to view them as dynamic, living systems with clear stages that roughly look like ours—birth, adolescence, maturity, and decline—with the added chance for rebirth rather than dissolution following decline.

One important point to remember about organizational life cycles, though, is that not all nonprofits move through all the typical stages. There is no time frame or rule that states that an organization must move into another stage of its life cycle after a period of years. A nonprofit may start up and move into the first stage of the life cycle and remain there for the rest of its existence. Or an organization may move through several stages and then find itself backtracking into an earlier stage. The process of life-cycle development in nonprofits is nonlinear.

Executive Directors are wise to assess the stage of life their nonprofits currently occupy. Different challenges and strengths characterize each stage in the life cycle of an organization. Each stage also may include shifts in organizational culture on what is valued and assumed, as well as differing policies and practices. Likewise, ED management and leadership priorities and skills must change to take advantage of the strengths and overcome the challenges.

This chapter helps you determine the life cycle stage your organization is in and provides you with helpful information on determining your role as Executive Director in each stage. It addresses these questions:

- What life cycle stage is my organization in?
- What skills does an Executive Director need in each stage?

What life cycle stage is my organization in?

There are many theories on organization life cycles. Most agree they follow the pattern of start-up, development, expansion, maturity, and crisis, followed by restructuring or decline. The chart in Exhibit 8.1 gives a description of each nonprofit life cycle stage and the strengths and challenges associated with it.

As you read through the chart, you may be thinking, "Well, we're a little bit of this stage and a little bit of that one." That means you are in a transition between stages. Or it may mean your nonprofit has actually stretched itself into a couple of different stages. That can happen too. If

Exhibit 8.1 Organization Life Cycle

Organization Stage	Organization Description
Start-up	Generally no paid staff; volunteers do all the work; Founder establishes the culture; heavy focus on getting programs started; lots of high energy and creativity.
Development	First staff hired (generally the ED), beginning of formalization with policies, job descriptions, structures; sometimes struggles over priorities and direction. A Founder who isn't in the ED role generally cuts back on activity or withdraws from the organization. Leadership is negotiated between Board and ED. Beginning of a new culture.
Expansion and growth	More staff hired; growth in programs and funding; early systems are outgrown and need replacing with formal ones; strategic planning and focus is a priority; boundaries between roles and authority of paid staff and volunteers set; Board expands and fully takes on governance role and ED has greater autonomy and authority. Culture shifts into settled mode.
Maturity	Growth levels off; formalized procedures are the norm; increased accountability and good relationships with funders; good financial management; sufficient funds. Viewed publicly as strong and stable organization.
Crisis and restructuring	Major change or crisis (internal or external) necessitates a major retooling. Frequent staff and board turnover lead to crisis-oriented planning; systems, structures, and programs are reevaluated and changed using new success criteria. New leaders bring change in style and sometimes in vision; lots of new creative energy. If successful, this stage leads to a new expansion and growth cycle; if unsuccessful, to decline and closing.
Decline and closing	Organizations are unable to make the changes needed to continue to operate. Focus is inward; personnel and board members withdraw; the organization suffers loss of funding and loss of public trust; programs cease or merger occurs.

you think this is the case for you, focus on the stage that has the most characteristics that match your organization. This is where your nonprofit is most grounded at the moment.

It's important to talk to others in your nonprofit to help answer this question. People have differing views on where their organization is depending on their position in the structure. Sharing these different perceptions among Board and staff members can lead to a rich discussion that is often educational for the Board, and sometimes eye-opening for staff as they hear the viewpoints of Board members!

Having these discussions with Board and staff may also help them understand the need for change in the nonprofit, or at least for doing some things in a different way. If you are in the middle of a change process in your organization, it's also helpful to reflect on where your nonprofit has been and what life cycle stage it is moving into.

Here is a process you can use with others to help determine what stage or transition period your nonprofit is currently in:

1. Have everyone reflect on the history, any changes that the organization has had, and previous accomplishments of the organization. List the significant accomplishments and periods of change in your history.

2. Ask people to identify the current strengths and challenges they think the nonprofit is facing. List the significant strengths and challenges.

3. Now show everyone the life cycle chart. Ask them to review the lists of historic changes and accomplishments and the strengths and challenges. Then have everyone individually choose a stage on the life cycle chart that they think most closely matches the data on the lists. There will probably be a variety of different choices.

4. Allow a full discussion to occur with each person's choice of position in the life cycle.

5. Narrow the possible stages to the one that is favored by the majority of the people participating in this exercise. This is most likely where your organization is in its life cycle.

6. If there is no clear majority opinion, then you may truly be in more than one stage.

What skills does an Executive Director need in each stage?

The ideal skill mix is a very important question for Executive Directors and for Boards who hire them. Too often Executive Directors find themselves with management or leadership skills that have become less valuable or less effective in the organization because it has shifted into a new stage. Understanding what new skills are most needed helps an Executive Director keep up with the organization.

Wisdom

Executive Directors must expand their skills or change their focus as their nonprofits move through the life cycle.

Story from the Field

A few years ago Mim worked with a nonprofit serving youth on a strategic planning process that was started because the organization had gone through a major growth period and was feeling fragmented. The Executive Director had spent twelve years as CEO of the nonprofit and another fifteen years in other positions. Basically, he grew up with the organization, starting as one of the youth served there.

In Mim's discussions with Board and staff about the strengths and weaknesses of the organization and priorities for the future, it quickly became evident that a major weakness was the Executive Director. Everyone felt terrible saying that he was a weak link in the organization because he had brought the nonprofit to its current position of strength. Unfortunately, people were worried that this individual was holding them back because of a limited set of leadership skills. The Board had a major concern about whether this Executive Director could really provide the skills needed for the nonprofit.

To address these concerns, Mim worked with the Board and staff to develop an understanding of what life cycle stage this organization was in, using the process described earlier in this chapter, as well as what skills the Executive Director lacked that were currently needed. Everyone also looked at what stage the organization might move to with their strategic plan and what skills the Executive Director would need in the future. Fortunately, the Executive Director was very open to developing new skills and went to work finding classes and books to retool himself for his nonprofit. Three years later the organization is thriving and the Executive Director is still there.

Clearly, it helps Executive Directors and nonprofits to know what stage the organization is in. Those EDs that successfully change themselves as the organization changes are the ones who ensure steady and strong leadership over a long period of time.

WARNING

If you find your organization is in the stage we call maturity, this is not the time to sit back and relax. Complacency is often the first step leading to the need for restructure or the start of the decline.

The chart in Exhibit 8.2 lists the specific leadership and management skills needed by Executive Directors for each stage in the life cycle. The five primary responsibilities (visionary, relationship builder, capacity creator, resource wizard, and change agent) are inherent in each stage. Obviously the complexity of applying these responsibilities increases as more staff, volunteers, and programs are added to an organization.

As you review the chart in the exhibit, reflect on what your organization decided its life cycle stage to be. Think about your own roles, responsibilities, and leadership focus or strengths as they relate to that stage. How do you match up with the requirements listed in the chart? The truth is that all skills are needed for each life cycle stage. However, in each stage some skills are most important to have. You may find that you need to develop new strengths or add to your skill sets if the organization is to thrive in its particular life stage—or at any rate, to make sure the organization

Exhibit 8.2 Executive Director Skills for Each Life Stage

Stage	Skills Needed
Start-up	• Program design • Visioning • Risk taking • Entrepreneurship
Development	• Systems development • Financial management and analysis • Program implementation • Board development
Expansion and growth	• Communication • Planning • Strategic thinking • Fundraising • Creating community • Change management
Maturity	• Delegation • Integration • Stabilization • Staff and board management • Partnership and collaboration
Crisis and restructuring	• Expansion stage skills • Adaptability • Acquisition of external resources
Decline and closing	• Communication • Planning • Financial management • Partnership and merger management

has these strengths and skills available. This can be done by your own professional development, through the addition of new staff, or bringing in new Board member expertise.

Exhibit 8.2 is also a useful resource for Board members seeking an Executive Director. They should use the leadership skills identified with their nonprofit's life cycle stage as criteria for hiring an individual who best fits the organization's requirements. As the chart is reviewed, Board members should keep in mind not just what is needed now in their nonprofit but what will be needed in the years ahead. If an organization is moving from one stage to another, it may be wiser to hire a new Executive Director whose skills suit the incoming stage.

Understanding your organization's life cycle stage is crucial in order to develop healthy change processes, as described in the next chapter. These life cycle stages are also directly affected by the external environment and how the sector itself is evolving. Executive Directors who have a good sense of changes happening, both internally and externally, are capable of being strategic and leading their nonprofits to success.

CHAPTER NINE

Leading Organizational Change

> *The most important things a leader can bring to a changing organization are passion, conviction, and confidence in others. Too often, executives announce a plan, launch a task force, and simply hope that people find the answers—instead of offering a dream, stretching their horizons, and encouraging people to do the same.*
> —ROSABETH MOSS KANTER, *The Enduring Skills of Change Leaders*

USUALLY THE PERSON WHO first realizes the need for a change in an organization is the Executive Director. It becomes the ED's job to manage change by first understanding the inherent tensions involved among those affected by any change taking place, and then by explaining to them the importance of changing organizational culture and doing things in a different way.

By saying this, we are not suggesting that the Executive Director is totally responsible for making change happen in a nonprofit. Being entrusted with the organization, the Executive Director is expected to know when a change is needed and to provide leadership. However, all successful organizational change stems from the

WARNING

Never begin a major change process until there is agreement by key stakeholders that change is needed. You may find that things are not as dire as originally stated and you may also get ideas on how to move forward.

Board, staff, and volunteers working together with the ED to make it happen. Thus, the Executive Director's role is to lead, manage, and support others (to work through others) for a healthy productive process.

Executive Directors often have doubts about the best way to move forward with a change process that affects the whole organization. This chapter addresses some of the key issues that Executive Directors have with organizational change and specifically answers the following questions:

Wisdom

Sustainable change requires vision, leadership, and buy-in.

- How can Executive Directors help their nonprofits embrace a healthy change process?
- What is the Executive Director's role and that of the Board, other staff, and volunteers in a change process?
- How soon after a new Executive Director is hired should a change process begin?

How can Executive Directors help their nonprofits embrace a healthy change process?

EDs are responsible for helping their nonprofits deal with organization-wide change, such as changing the focus of the mission, arranging a merger, making major programmatic changes that affect people and systems inside the organization as well as clients, or moving to a new Executive Director.

Most theories of successful organization change processes suggest the following elements:

- A trusted leader (the ED) with a bold vision that creates excitement for change throughout the organization.
- Visible and committed Board and staff leadership that is present during all phases of the change process.

- Clear and consistent communication at all levels and throughout the entire process to make sure everyone knows what is happening and why.

- Understanding that resistance is normal and should be handled constructively. People embrace change at different rates and with different responses.

- System-wide thinking that enables people to see that making a change in one part of the organization is going to affect other areas.

- A concrete plan of action for the change process with measures that allow everyone to see and celebrate success as it occurs.

If you are an Executive Director contemplating an organization-wide change, it is important to address the elements listed here before you start. If they are not in place, you may want to spend some time preparing the organization before moving forward. Having these elements in place becomes even more important if you must move your organization quickly through change on a regular basis because of some crisis in the organization.

WARNING

If you start too soon with a change process or leave out some important voices in your decision to move forward, you face an uphill battle to gain support and overcome resistance to the process once it has begun.

Once a foundation for change is in place, you can begin to lead people through the series of steps in the change process illustrated in Exhibit 9.1. While these steps appear to be linear, understand they are not. People's response to change in any organization requires moving backward and forward throughout the process. To be successful, the Executive Director and other leaders in the process must stay aware of the concerns, emotions, and other resistance from those who are affected by the change. As you move through the process, steps may need to be revisited to ensure buy-in and ultimate success.

The process outlined in Exhibit 9.1 will work if you and other leaders stay very visible and available to help people through the early days

Exhibit 9.1 Change Process

Step One: *Envision.* Provide a compelling need for change and a picture of what can be. This often includes the potential risks of not changing as well as the benefits of changing. Create a compelling vision statement that depicts what the organization will look like if the change process is successful. Include Board members, key staff, and volunteers in this process of envisioning. To move to the next step, you need their commitment to both the need for change and the vision for the new state of the organization.

Step Two: *Communicate.* Share the case for change with all staff and volunteers and with the consumers who will be most affected by the changes taking place. Don't expect full commitment to the vision immediately, but you should see excitement and interest before moving on.

Step Three: *Set Goals.* Make the vision concrete with specific goals created by key leaders in your organization. For instance, if you are contemplating adding new programs and your vision is of an organization doubled in size, providing a continuum of comprehensive programs to a broader consumer group, then you could have goals along these lines:

1. In one year, technology and communication systems to support the organization's growth will be in place.

2. In two years, new programs will be fully integrated.

3. In three years, XX additional clients will be served.

Broad acceptance of the goals is essential before it's safe to move to the next step.

Step Four: *Define Roles.* Develop an action plan with Board and staff participation to achieve the goals. Lead your Board and staff in determining the roles to be played by the individuals in your organization. Share the action plan with everyone so that staff, Board, volunteers, and key consumers understand that the process of change is well planned, and that they have a role in making it happen. This understanding is crucial before actual implementation begins.

Exhibit 9.1 Change Process (continued)

Step Five: *Benchmark Progress.* Set benchmarks in the plan that will enable you to measure progress, keep implementation focused, reevaluate processes, and celebrate success. For instance, with the goals listed in Step Three, you might have a benchmark for five months that states that a community needs assessment has been completed that identifies the new programs to be developed.

Step Six: *Take Action.* Put your organization's action plan into operation. It is important throughout this time to fully communicate how things are progressing with individuals in the organization. When resistance from individuals arises, handle it with compassion, remembering that change is difficult, but also with firmness and confidence that the vision you are working toward is best for the organization.

Step Seven: *Establish Learning Opportunities.* Concurrently with step six, create new learning opportunities for staff who find their jobs evolving as change takes place. Consider these questions:

- Do some staff need new skills to do their new jobs more effectively?

- Are communication patterns going to change and is there a need to provide some training to help staff work better together?

- Is the Board's role going to expand and do they need training to be able to provide new governance for the organization?

Step Eight: *Celebrate.* Although you have been celebrating successes throughout the change process, be sure to arrange a major celebration when the process is completed. This has been hard work and everyone needs a pat on the back for making it happen!

Step Nine: *Emotional Check-Up.* After the action plan is implemented, continue to monitor how well people are adjusting. Make sure the change is having the impact originally envisioned. And remember that resistance will reappear as people realize "the good old days" are really over.

of the changed organization. It is also the Executive Director's responsibility to regularly communicate positive impacts that are occurring due to the change during and after implementation, as well as to acknowledge new challenges that emerge.

What is the Executive Director's role and that of the Board, other staff, and volunteers in a change process?

Your role as Executive Director is to be the change leader. You are the person who inspires, motivates, and leads change toward the vision you have articulated. You are also a key manager and work to ensure that communication processes are working, and that change is happening. Finally, you are a supporter and follower. In this capacity, you provide support to others in the organization who are doing their part to lead the process.

Wisdom

Before launching a major organization-wide change as an Executive Director new to the nonprofit, make sure all parties affected have been talked to, and all voices heard.

Your Board members are your partners in the change process. They provide support with expert advice, strategic thinking, and planning. In a sense, it is the Board's job to keep the big-picture perspective—to be thinking about ways the change will affect the community being served. Board members should also be discussing among themselves how their roles may need to change as a result of the process.

However, one change process requires the Board to take the responsibility of change leader. That is the hiring of a new Executive Director. This is probably one of the most important responsibilities of the Board of Directors, and one that cannot be delegated to staff. Hiring an Executive Director generally has an impact on the whole organization. This is an exciting change for any nonprofit and one where Boards can show strong leadership. We discuss Executive Director transitions in greater detail in Chapter Eighteen.

Among Board and staff, some will be leaders who, with the Executive Director, will be able to inspire others and communicate progress. When change involves the institution or dissolution of a program or implementation of new technology, all staff should also participate in making the change happen. In the end, staff members should be involved in planning any change that affects their work. They should also be kept informed of progress toward the new vision every step of the way.

How soon after a new Executive Director is hired should a change process begin?

The answer to this question is the classic "It depends." If an Executive Director new to the nonprofit discovers a dire situation, then change needs to happen immediately. An organization facing bankruptcy, lawsuits over employment practices, or threats of funder cutbacks unless it makes some programmatic or organizational change must do something right away, and so must one suffering from an unhealthy culture that has people stuck or in constant conflict.

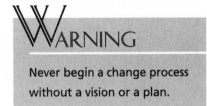

WARNING

Never begin a change process without a vision or a plan.

In situations where you must implement a change process within a few months after being hired, it becomes imperative to identify other leaders in the organization who can help you formulate, articulate, and lead the vision, and set the course for achieving it. Executive Directors new to an organization need strong allies, particularly during tough times. A change process can help to create these allies and forge partnerships that will support and sustain you for years after the change is completed.

If no major crises are facing the organization when you arrive, we recommend waiting a minimum of six months into the job before beginning discussions about any organization-wide change. Remember that one key criterion to a successful change process is a compelling need, and your vision for what the change can do. It takes time to develop this vision. No change process should begin until you, the Board, and key staff have a very clear understanding of the need for change and the vision to bring it to life.

Also, this time period gives you, the new person in the organization, a chance to build trust with Board and staff members. You also have some time to take a hard look at what change might be needed and to gather information from key stakeholders.

PART FOUR

Executive Director as Relationship Builder

Relationships of trust depend on our willingness to look not only to our own interests, but also the interests of others.

—PETER FARQUHARSON

ONE OF THE CHARACTERISTICS that separate the truly great Executive Directors from the simply good ones is the ability to build strong relationships that benefit the organization. To do this, you must be a powerful communicator, believe in the beauty of teamwork and collaboration, be genuinely curious about and engaging with everyone you meet, and carry the respect of your community.

Relationship building is not always an easy task for the busy Executive Director. New EDs who are used to doing the work in other jobs often struggle with the fact that the Executive Director most often works through others to accomplish something. This is one of the most important concepts for an Executive Director to learn. The job is not about doing things, it is about leading, managing, and supporting others through relationships.

In this section of the Survival Guide, Chapters Ten and Eleven describe effective relationship-building strategies with Board members and paid and unpaid staff. The focus of these chapters is to provide you with ideas and tools to find your own level of ease and satisfaction while inspiring others to work together and be productive.

Chapter Twelve focuses on working with Founders or following in their footsteps. There are special challenges associated with filling the shoes of the visionary who started the organization. It helps to build a solid relationship with the Founder.

CHAPTER TEN

Nurturing a Relationship with the Board

If all nonprofit Boards focused on the mission, did not allow individual agendas and personalities to overwhelm the collective needs of the organization, and worked in partnership to define the organization's future, a great deal of dysfunction would disappear from the nonprofit sector.

—Deborah Linnell, Zora Radosevich, and Jonathan Spack, *Executive Director's Guide*

WE HAVE FOUND in our years of nonprofit work that the single most important factor in determining the success of a Board is how well it partners with the Executive Director. If the relationship is healthy, the organization thrives. If the relationship is unstable or poor, the organization suffers.

In this chapter, we explore what makes a healthy relationship between a Board and its Executive Director by answering the following questions:

• What are the attributes of an effective Board and what does it take to create one?

- What does a healthy relationship between a Board and its Executive Director look like and how is it established?
- How does one differentiate between Board and Executive Director responsibilities?
- What information does the Board need, and how often?
- Who makes what decisions in a nonprofit?
- How important is the relationship between the Executive Director and the Board Chair?
- What do you do if there are problems between you and the Board Chair?
- What should an Executive Director do with a renegade Board member?

What are the attributes of an effective Board and what does it take to create one?

A tremendous amount of research has been done on the question of Board effectiveness—libraries of books, articles, research papers, interviews, newsletters, and other materials have been developed to help non-profit Boards do their work better. Yet a great many Executive Directors wonder why they need a Board at all, because in their experience very little about the Board's role adds value to their organization.

The most important point in all the literature on Boards of Directors is that the effective Board is one with the following attributes:

- A focus on and passion for the organization's mission and a commitment to setting and achieving the vision.
- A set of clear responsibilities that keep the Board away from any possibility of micromanagement.
- A desire to work together as a group, to listen to divergent viewpoints, and to build consensus.

- A structure that is flexible and changes to fit the life cycle and priorities of the organization.

- An understanding of, and the ability to help shape, the organization's culture.

- An interest in being informed about the good, bad, and uncertain in the nonprofit, and a willingness to analyze and resolve issues that are within their purview.

- A commitment to self-reflection and evaluation, with expectations clearly stated and each person accountable to meet them.

No one-size-fits-all formula can make every Board of Directors effective. Similarly, no one model will work equally well for all Boards. Creating an effective Board requires hard work by the Board members and Executive Director, and it happens over a long time.

With that said, it is useful to know several different models of Board effectiveness and use them as a frame of reference for determining what might work for your own Board of Directors. Many groups mix and match between these and other models. A number of hybrids are extremely effective. Determining what works often requires a trial-and-error approach that evolves over time into your own unique model. The chart in Exhibit 10.1 describes some of the current popular models. All of them contain some wisdom, but your organization needs to choose or build one that best fits its culture and needs.

Using the models in Exhibit 10.1 as a frame of reference, Executive Directors can work with Board leadership on a process to move the Board of Directors toward effectiveness. Generally speaking, it is not a good idea to travel this road alone as the Executive Director. You need commitment on the part of some of the Board leadership to change and become more effective, or no change will occur. Exhibit 10.2 provides a good example of how to move a Board toward greater effectiveness.

Wisdom

A well-defined partnership between the Board and the Executive Director is central to sustainability and effectiveness of both the ED and the organization.

Exhibit 10.1 Board Roles and Responsibilities Models

Creator	Overview	Key Board Responsibilities
Cyril Houle	Boards Make Policy, Staff Implement It Model	• Create and monitor the mission. • Develop policies. • Develop long-range plans. • Evaluate programs. • Hire and work with the Executive Director. • Arbitrate conflict among staff. • Fulfill the legal responsibilities of the nonprofit. • Secure adequate financing and manage it well. • Make the organization visible in the community. • Evaluate itself.
John Carver	Policy Governance Model	• *Ends:* Determination of which needs are to be met, for whom, and at what cost (a Board role). • *Executive Limitations:* Determination of the boundaries within which the Board and staff operate to establish methods and activities to reach the ends (a Board and ED role). • *Board-Staff Linkage:* Determination of the authority delegated to the Executive Director and how that person's performance will be evaluated (Board and ED role). • *Board Governance:* Determination of the Board's philosophy, accountability, and the specifics of its job (a Board role).
Karl Mathiasen	Board Passages Model	Board life cycle stages: • *Organizing:* Boards of Directors consist of volunteers who follow a founding leader, or who collectively run the organization. • *Governing:* Boards of Directors move from doing all the work of the organization to performing only governance functions. • *Mature:* Boards of Directors perform largely a fundraising role in a nonprofit, both in giving and asking.

Exhibit 10.1 Board Roles and Responsibilities Models (continued)

Creator	Overview	Key Board Responsibilities
Richard Chait	New Work of the Board Model	Model looks at Board member impact and process. Specifically, • Boards must add value to their nonprofit. This will look different in every organization. • Board members should become involved in those issues that really matter to the nonprofit and take action right alongside the staff. • Boards need a flexible structure to change as quickly as the organization does.
Robert Herman	Board-Centered Leadership Model	Executive Director is central focus of the nonprofit and leads the Board in the following areas: • Defining the direction of the organization. • Ensuring the effectiveness of programs. • Key decision making right alongside the Board. • Collaboration on most governance issues. In addition, the Executive Director is evaluated partially on the quality of leadership given to the Board and organization.
Diane Duca and Candace Widmer	Model for All-Volunteer Organizations	The Board is in the position of being more involved in the direct operations of the organization because it has no staff members. Boards with this model have the following characteristics: • Board members are service providers, program coordinators, fundraisers, and administrators. • Board members have a good understanding of the intricacies of the organization, determine policies, and carry them out. • Board members are deeply dedicated to the cause and often reflect a grassroots orientation to solving community problems.

Exhibit 10.2 Building an Effective Board

Step One: Spend time as a Board of Directors discussing the organization's culture and where it is in its life cycle. (You can do this by using process examples given in Chapters Four and Eight, which address these topics.) This is a step that provides a grounding for moving forward.

Step Two: Make sure the Board members know and understand the mission and vision of the organization. If any of them do not, the Board needs educating on these topics.

Step Three: Clarify the organization's priorities and critical issues. Discuss individual members' interest in meeting those priorities and resolving the issues.

Step Four: Create a list of mutually agreed-upon Board responsibilities and expectations for the coming year that reflect the life cycle stage, culture, and priorities of the organization.

Step Five: Prepare a commitment form for each Board member to sign that states their willingness to be accountable for meeting the responsibilities and expectations. Members who choose not to sign the commitment form should be excused from the Board and thanked for their service.

Step Six: Develop Board goals that will allow it to fulfill the responsibilities and help to meet the priorities.

Step Seven: Form committees, based on individual interest, that will complete the goals.

Step Eight: Establish a regular schedule to check on committee work (at every Board meeting or once a quarter) and a Board evaluation process for completing the goals.

Note: While many packaged Board evaluation forms are on the market, it's best for the Board and Executive Director to develop and use a form tailored to the organization.

This process cannot be completed in a one-day retreat or as part of a few Board meetings. A retreat may be the starting point, but the Board should expect to have ongoing conversations over time. Also, it is important to realize that the process outlined in the exhibit only partially leads to a more effective Board. Working well together as a group may result from the effort. However, we encourage additional work on team building, consensus decision making, and meeting management to strengthen the group.

Here is an example of how one nonprofit used the process described in Exhibit 10.2 to make their Board more effective:

Story from the Field

An Executive Director—new to her organization and to the profession—found herself with a Board of four people who were primarily interested in helping the staff run their programs. This new ED was following on the heels of a very strong Founder who had used the Board primarily as adjunct program volunteers and had not seen the need for them to take on a governance role.

The first thing the Executive Director did was have a candid conversation with her Board Chair about the importance of Board members providing governance rather than assisting staff. She shared materials about what Boards do and how they can add value. The Board Chair agreed that their governance tasks had gone awry. They both agreed that new Board membership was needed to build the Board, that training was needed for everyone, and that part of the training should include ways to be accountable to the organization and the community served.

Finally, the Board Chair and the ED wanted the experience for all members to be fun as well as educational.

A recruitment campaign was held to find a minimum of four new Board members who had skills not currently present, and some who had served on other nonprofit Boards. After a few months, the new members were voted in, and a day-long orientation was held.

With all five staff present, the Board reviewed the mission statement, discussed the next year's program, fundraising, and administrative priorities (they had no strategic plan), and talked about their interests in serving on the Board as well as their skills. In the end, the Board talked about how they could individually and collectively add the greatest value to the organization as it entered a heavy growth stage in its life cycle. They also talked about how they wanted to work together as a group, and what they expected from each other.

Wisdom

Roles, responsibilities, authority, and expectations of the Board and ED should be clearly spelled out and reviewed at minimum on an annual basis.

Following the meeting, and over the next several months, the conversations at the retreat were shaped into a list of responsibilities and expectations and a work plan. This work was done by a subset of the Board and the Executive Director. Committees were formed as the work plan was approved. It was agreed that each committee would establish its own tasks, and report on progress at each quarterly Board meeting.

Developing the Board's effectiveness continues to be a high priority for the Chair and Executive Director. Meetings consist of exercises to create cohesiveness as well as ongoing education on the nonprofit's work in the community.

The success of this organization results from the Board members' recognition that they could be more effective—and that they needed to be more effective—for the organization to thrive. Their own passion for the mission and desire to be of value sustained them through a long process and some very long meetings.

What does a healthy relationship between a Board and its Executive Director look like and how is it established?

Imagine this. Your Board of Directors meets regularly with a planned agenda established by the Board Chair with your advice. Committees are active and doing important work. Discussion and decisions are based on the knowledge Board members have about their roles and responsibilities in the organization, and on the voiced expectations they have for each other. As you sit in the meeting with them, you see each person engaged in the decision making and everyone actively accepting responsibility for their work. Board members ask you, the Executive Director, what support you need from them, and you feel safe enough to honestly and directly answer this question and the others that they ask you. The whole tone of the meeting is one of mutual trust and respect for one another as well as a genuine desire to be in a solid partnership with you.

WARNING

Never think of the Board as an unnecessary hindrance to the organization.

This is what a healthy Board-ED relationship looks like. And, like all relationships, it involves constant work, attention, honesty, and continuous nurturing to survive and thrive.

Here are the qualities that form a healthy Board-ED relationship.

For the Board of Directors

- Board members know their responsibilities; they are neither micromanaging the organization nor absent from it.

- Board members express their expectations to one another regarding commitment, participation, and level of activity.

- Board members express their expectations to the Executive Director regarding communication, management style, leadership style, or other relevant behaviors.

- Board members participate willingly and work actively in areas of their strengths.

- Board members have realistic expectations for the ED regarding communication, management style, leadership style, and other relevant behaviors.

- Board members have enough information to feel knowledgeable and engaged.

- Board members feel trusted, respected, and viewed as a partner by the Executive Director. In turn, they value, trust, and respect the ED.

For the Executive Director

- The Executive Director is willing to share the good, the bad, and the uncertain with Board members without fear of reprisal or blame. Information is shared on an ongoing basis with the philosophy of no surprises.
- The Executive Director, with the Board, establishes clear lines of decision-making authority.
- The Executive Director is quick to ask for help when needed, and seeks advice or support from Board members.
- The Executive Director sees the value of shared or collaborative leadership with the Board.
- The Executive Director expresses expectations to the Board in a positive, constructive way that is also realistic.
- The Executive Director provides support as needed and makes the work of the Board a priority.

These lists of qualities can be distilled into a list of the four essential ingredients for creating a healthy relationship between you and your Board: clear communication, clear decision-making authority, clear roles and responsibilities, and clear criteria for success. In other words, you and your Board must have agreement on these questions:

- Who does what?
- What information do the Board and the ED need?
- Who makes what decisions?
- What does success look like for the Board/ED relationship?

Every organization will answer these questions differently depending on the unique partnership that exists. For many, the answers will involve some blurred areas. In all cases, the healthy partnership is a dance that evolves over time—and toes sometimes get stepped on. When this happens, it is important to talk about what happened and mutually decide on a better way to work together.

How does one differentiate between Board and Executive Director responsibilities?

An example of how one Board and Executive Director sorted out their respective responsibilities is described in Exhibit 10.3. They decided they had some shared activities, and some where either the ED or the Board should take the lead. This is just an example. The chart may be used as a tool for starting discussion with your Board to bring clarity to who does what.

Exhibit 10.3 describes a division of labor that works best for a group with a paid Executive Director. Organizations in the start-up or development stage may not have someone with the designated title of ED, in which case all Board members share in all the activities needed for success. As an organization moves from having Board members handle many of the day-to-day program and administrative responsibilities to having them provide an oversight role, some tensions can arise. Board members who have been the doers may not like giving up that responsibility to become the trustees. Executive Director leadership is needed to make a smooth transition. Board members should not be expected to slip into their new responsibilities comfortably overnight, and the Executive Director should work with Board members to clarify their new role in the organization and identify the steps members should take to move into that role. The exhibit can be helpful at that point in providing a clear picture of who does what.

One good way to clarify who does what is to have an Executive Director work plan. Boards of Directors need goals to strive toward, and so do Executive Directors. Ideally, the ED and Board goals will be closely coordinated to clarify responsibilities, expectations, accountability, and areas where support is needed.

Many ED work plans have performance objectives that state what the Executive Director must do to be successful in the Board's collective mind.

Wisdom

Boardsmanship comes in a variety of styles, so don't search for the one perfect model for governance. Every nonprofit needs to determine what is most effective for its organizational culture and life cycle stage.

Exhibit 10.3 Sample Board-ED Partnership

Activity	Board of Directors	Executive Director	Both
Relationship Building			
• Build and sustain organization culture			Share
• Board team building	Lead	Support	
• Board meeting management	Lead	Support	
• Board recruitment and orientation	Lead	Support	
• Board development and assessment	Lead	Support	
• Hiring, assessment, and removal of Executive Director	Lead	Support	
• Hiring staff and volunteers	Support	Lead	
• Staff development and assessment	Support	Lead	
• Staff and volunteer team building	Support	Lead	
• Staff and volunteer recognition			Share
Community Creator			
• Build community partnerships	Support	Lead	
• Raise organizational visibility			Share
• Ensure broad representation			Share
• Build a multicultural organization			Share
Visioning—and Planning			
• Ensure mission-based decisions	Lead	Support	
• Create organizational vision	Support	Lead	
• Establish organization priorities			Share
• Develop operations policies	Support	Lead	
• Monitor strategic plan's accomplishments	Lead	Support	
• Develop and assess programs	Support	Lead	

Exhibit 10.3 Sample Board-ED Partnership (continued)

Activity	Board of Directors	Executive Director	Both
Resource Development			
• Create fundraising plans			Share
• Cultivate and ask major donors	Lead	Support	
• Develop and analyze annual fund	Support	Lead	
• Build funder relationships			Share
• Develop annual budgets	Support	Lead	
• Prepare financial reports	Support	Lead	
• Monitor budgets and finances	Lead	Support	
Change Agent			
• Develop and manage organization change processes	Support	Lead	
• Create and manage executive transition process	Lead	Support	

Note: Lead = Overall responsibility and accountability; makes sure the job gets done

Share= Agreed-upon leadership responsibilities and accountability for each

Support= Provide information, expertise, assistance to get the job done

Exhibit 10.4 shows an example of an Executive Director's work plan with performance objectives. It comes from an organization that has a few staff people with program responsibilities, as well as a support staff person.

Clear performance objectives and defined responsibilities make good communication much easier. Board members understand what the Executive Director is doing and what communication is needed to help ensure success.

Exhibit 10.4 Sample Executive Director
Work Plan and Performance Objectives

	Target Date

Fundraising Performance Goals

- Increase grant revenues by 15 percent by fiscal year end.

- Increase nongovernmental revenues by 10 percent this fiscal year.

- Receive major donor level gifts from five people (with Board leadership).

Professional development needs: A course in proposal writing

Staff Management Performance Goals

- Improve supervisor skills in evaluating their staff with two trainings by HR specialists.

- Conduct an evaluation of staff morale and report results to Board.

Professional development needs: Coaching on managing diverse staff and volunteers

Board Development Goals

- Support the recruitment of four new Board members.

- Develop a Board orientation program.

- Schedule a program manager to speak at quarterly Board meetings.

Vision Goals

- Lead Board and staff in a process to redefine organizational vision.

- Communicate the organizational vision to constituency audiences through a minimum of five speaking engagements.

What information does the Board need, and how often?

We've been on Boards where we were just swamped with information, all of it good but probably not all necessary. We've also served on Boards where we had to drag the most basic information out of the Executive Director. Neither situation is desirable. So what is a good balance?

At the very least, here is what Board members should receive from an Executive Director on a monthly basis:

- *An update:* A two- or three-page paper that describes what is going on at your organization, including successes and challenges
- *Financials:* Reports that present monthly and year-to-date revenues and expenditures compared to budget, along with an explanation for any major discrepancies, and a balance sheet
- *Fund development status:* A list of grants mailed and received, major donor gifts received and recognition given, and any other important activity related to fundraising
- *Community creation:* An update on efforts to build the visibility of the organization and its partnerships
- *Background information needed for decisions:* Written summaries that communicate options with pros and cons for any decision a Board has to make

If Board members have all this information well in advance of a meeting (at least five days prior) they generally have time to become informed. When Board members are well informed, they are apt to become more involved and to trust the Executive Director's leadership.

Communication between the Board and Executive Director is particularly important when the organization is facing a crisis. For example, your nonprofit may be unable to make payroll because of cash flow problems. Or an article is about to appear in the newspaper that presents a negative view of your organization. Or a former employee has filed a lawsuit. Whatever the crisis, you should inform the Board before it becomes public knowledge. This may necessitate a quick e-mail for a small crisis, a phone call to explain a more serious impending problem, or an emergency meeting under the direst of circumstances.

Executive Directors may feel anything from mild apprehension to full-blown terror when faced with informing a Board of a crisis situation. Regardless, those Executive Directors who are slow to communicate with their Boards often face larger problems when Board members find out from other sources. Wondering why you did not tell them what was happening, Board members are likely to put the worst spin on events, become suspicious, and lose trust in you. Rebuilding this trust can be very difficult and time-consuming.

Remember also, that Board members are partners with you in your capacity as Executive Director, and as partners they have much to contribute to finding the solution. We've known many Executive Directors who felt they couldn't go to the Board with their problems or who became fearful during a crisis because they thought they would be blamed for the problem. Finger pointing has never solved a problem or prevented a crisis. Focusing on finding solutions is critical to a healthy Board-ED relationship.

WARNING

Never withhold information from the Board that they request or need to make effective decisions.

Who makes what decisions in a nonprofit?

A healthy Board-ED relationship also involves clear understanding of who makes what decisions. It's much more complicated than "Board decides this, ED decides that." It's also often not enough to say that the Executive Director makes all day-to-day decisions while the Board makes policy decisions. For most groups, the lines blur. A more efficient way of thinking about decision-making structure is to divide decision making into Board Executive Committee decisions, Board of Directors decisions, and Executive Director decisions.

For instance, you and your Board may conclude that the Board Executive Committee has the authority to decide on the following:

- Steps to take in an immediate crisis
- Any decision that must be made between Board meetings that does not involve changing the structure, by-laws, budget, or Executive Director

The full Board may have authority for the following decisions:

- Selection of new Board members
- Hiring and firing of the Executive Director
- Selection of the auditor
- Setting the mission and vision for the organization
- Defining policies on overspending the budget, accepting controversial donations, human resources, new programs and abolishing established ones, and other choices likely to affect the direction or character of the organization
- Purchasing or selling a building or other capital asset

The Executive Director may have authority for these decisions:

- Hiring and firing of staff and volunteers
- Developing program design and implementation strategies
- Developing fundraising strategy, including selection of prospects and of individuals to build connections with them
- Identifying best candidates for partnerships and strategic collaborations
- Preparing annual staff plans and performance criteria
- Making routine contracts and setting day-to-day policies for operations, financial management, and evaluation procedures

These lists are not exhaustive, nor should they be viewed as the only way to delineate decision-making authority. Having job descriptions, written expectations, and work plans for the ED helps in determining who makes what decisions.

Here's an example of how a group grappled with and resolved a decision-making issue. A thirty-member Board of Directors was presented with an agenda item to approve a contract for a large planning grant. The Board Chair and Executive Director asked for the approval without presenting any background information on the contract. Board members balked at giving approval and questions were raised about who should be making new contract decisions. The ED realistically said that if he had to get Board approval for every contract, it would take forever with this size Board. On the other hand, Board members wanted to know what they were getting the organization into—a wise perspective to take!

The Board asked the Executive Director to present them with a summary of the contract via e-mail. They decided that if e-mail discussion showed everyone to be in favor of the contract, they would go forward. If consensus could not be reached, the Board agreed to attend a special meeting for further discussion and decision making. They also agreed that the ED should decide on all contracts not affecting agency direction.

The situation in this story would have been easier to deal with had the Board and ED had a clear understanding of authority on signing contracts. This can be done through a contract approval policy that spells out the types of contracts an ED can sign and the financial limits.

It becomes crucial to take time to orient new Board members into the delicate decision-making structure you have established, so that they can

Wisdom

Building a strong relationship with your Board Chair is a key step to a strong partnership with your Board of Directors.

quickly adjust to your organization's way of working together. Thus a Board orientation becomes much more than providing the history, program information, and financial data of your nonprofit. It's also about all the subjects of this chapter. Remaining attentive to the relationship between you and your Board up front and particularly as new members join the Board can save you many headaches and heartaches down the road.

How important is the relationship between the Executive Director and the Board Chair?

We usually hear questions about the importance of the relationship from either a Chair or an Executive Director when the two are having trouble dealing with each other. The short answer is that there is no more important relationship in your non-profit than the one between the Executive Director and Board Chair. If these two leaders are not aligned, it often spells disaster. On the other hand, when they are working cohesively together, the whole organization usually enjoys harmony and progress.

> **WARNING**
>
> Never risk being the second to bring your Board bad news.

It's very important for an Executive Director who is new to an organization to get off to a good start with the current Board Chair. One way to do this is to have a conversation about what the Chair expects from you, and vice versa. This conversation should also include the development of a social contract, formal or informal, that indicates how frequently you will meet for sharing information, getting advice, and so on, and also gives details on how you and your Board Chair want to communicate with each other. Any time you have a new Board Chair, be sure to go through this process again. Never assume that what worked for one person is going to work for another.

In most situations, maintaining a harmonious relationship between you and the Board Chair is not that difficult. Here are some ideas that you might want to include in a social contract:

- *Regular meetings.* By phone or in person, it's useful for the two of you to discuss any current or emerging issues and consider how to mobilize Board and staff if needed. You can also update each other on the organization as you see it—and take some time to just have fun together, which is the best way to cement a working relationship.

- *No surprises.* Both the Chair and the Executive Director should lock into their brains the concept that anything one knows about something that is going to affect the organization needs to be communicated to the other.

The importance of regular communications and the prevention of surprises applies to everything that happens, from mundane issues like the heat wasn't working for two days and now staff is upset to the much more important events like the loss of major funding support that challenge organizational survival. Sometimes EDs don't tell their Board Chairs about truly day-to-day operating issues because they think that it isn't the Board's responsibility to be involved. But providing information is not the same as a request to become actively involved in solving the problem. You may not want your Chair to bother thinking how to get the heat back on. You've probably got that one figured out. However, you need to remember that if there are problems anywhere in your organization, people are talking about them and word is going to get to the Board. It's generally best to be the first to let your Chair know about an issue—that way you'll have the Chair's support (or at least know how the Chair will react) when the inevitable complaint makes its way up the line.

What do you do if there are problems between you and the Board Chair?

It is best for you to take the first step to proffer the olive branch to a difficult Board Chair. Remember that your Board Chair is a volunteer and needs to be recognized and valued for giving time and effort freely to your organization. Here is one way you can take to establish or reestablish a good relationship. Ask for a meeting to "clear the air." At that meeting, use the following approach:

- Reestablish the common ground of your mutual passion for the mission of your organization.
- Explain how the difficulties between the two of you are hurting what you both are passionate about.
- Use "I" statements to describe how you feel, how you see that you may have contributed to the situation at hand, and what you need from the Board Chair to have a more positive relationship.
- Ask the Board Chair for a similar description of feelings and needs relating to the current situation. In all of this, your goal is to negotiate to a win-win for both of you.
- Reaffirm or establish expectations you have of each other in the areas of communication, decision making, and supporting each other.

Most of the time, a good honest conversation will bring you closer together again. If you are not able to resolve a situation, then involve another Board member (believe us, they know you and the Board Chair aren't getting along even if you're both sure you've been hiding the fact). Sometimes it may be necessary to involve an outside person who can listen objectively to the feelings and needs of both of you and possibly offer suggestions for mending the relationship.

If all else fails, it is probably best for the Board Chair, as volunteer, to resign from the position and let someone who can work with the Executive Director step in.

What should an Executive Director do with a renegade Board member?

Renegade Board members come in several varieties. There's the Board member who calls the Executive Director and gives direction on matters that are the purview of the whole Board, not just one member. Or the one who goes to staff, bypassing the Executive Director, and gives direction to them. Or the one who disagrees with the group on some issue and proceeds to follow a private course of action rather than the one chosen by the Board.

Every Executive Director has had run-ins with people like these. They are generally well intentioned and have no idea they cause such problems for an organization. However, the unmanaged renegade Board member can become a real nightmare for the nonprofit and the Executive Director.

The first thing to remember is that the Executive Director is not responsible for renegade Board members. The Board holds that responsibility. When you believe that a Board member has been out of line, the best first step is to contact the Board Chair. If, by some unfortunate circumstance, the renegade is the Board Chair, then contact the Vice-Chair. Talk over the situation with your Board leader and let that person do something to stop whatever action the renegade member is engaging in. Most of the time, a quick phone call or meeting between the Board Chair and that member is all that is needed. More often than not, individuals don't know they are out of line and just need a reminder.

Occasionally, you may get some valuable feedback out of a conversation with a renegade Board member. The Board member may not have had enough information to understand that a course of action taken was inappropriate or could be problematic. Or perhaps the Board member went off on a tangent as a result of feeling out of the loop. Getting to the bottom of the renegade Board member's behavior is the best way to put an end to it.

Many Boards of Directors have consumers of the nonprofit's services as members. This heightens the possibility of someone taking action on a matter that might be personally important to them, as a consumer, without waiting for Board determination on the best course of action for the organization to follow.

In training sessions with Boards that have consumers among the members, we always talk about the "two-hat theory." This theory sets the boundaries by which a consumer knows when to act in a Board capacity (first hat), and when to act as a consumer (second hat). The following story provides an example of this situation.

Mim recently conducted a training with a Board where more than half of the members were parents of children who attended the camp run by the nonprofit. Like all other consumers of this camp, they wanted it to be an ideal experience for their children. Unfortunately, this often meant that a consumer Board member would go directly to counselors or the camp director and tell them what they were supposed to be doing. Staff members would be reminded that it was a Board member talking, and action needed to happen quickly! On one occasion, staff received totally opposite instructions from two Board members! Furthermore, both sets of instructions differed from what the Executive Director was asking the staff to do, as well as from what they themselves thought was best for the children. They were caught in an impossible situation and were left feeling frustrated and unable to make good decisions.

The two-hat theory helped the parents see that when they were at camp, they were consumers and could ask staff to make changes, the same as any other consumer. They should expect staff to go to the Executive Director with their ideas, just as staff would do with any consumer idea. Any request needing Board action would be brought to the Board, where a decision would be made and all Board members were expected to abide by that decision. The staff heaved a visible sigh of relief upon hearing this explanation! And the Board members also accepted it because it helped them understand the problems of taking action individually rather than as a group.

In this example, some of the parent Board members had gone renegade. It took some clear setting of boundaries and a better understanding of Board responsibilities to remind the group that they were to make decisions as a group and then live by those decisions.

We have covered a lot of ground in this chapter. The bottom line is the importance of having a healthy relationship between you and your Board of Directors, and especially between you and your Board Chair. If you take the time to make sure you have mutually understood responsibilities and expectations, good communication systems, and a clear process for decision making, then you have taken the essential steps toward a healthy and happy partnership.

CHAPTER ELEVEN

Establishing Productive Staff Relationships

Almost no one is going to have the luxury of working alone. All of us are going to be working in ways in which we're interdependent with other people. The only way we can do that effectively is to build competence in relationships.

—MAX DE PREE, *Leading Without Power*

A WISE EXECUTIVE DIRECTOR views an organization as a community of people with diverse talents, ideas, beliefs, and interests. Within this community, the Executive Director wears many hats from moment to moment: manager, leader, mentor, coach, team player, or follower. Understanding what hat is needed in interactions with paid and unpaid (volunteer) staff is an important skill to have and is crucial to building and maintaining good relationships.

This chapter suggests answers to the following questions that Executive Directors ask about working with staff and volunteers:

- How does an Executive Director who is new to an organization build quick credibility with paid and unpaid staff?

- How does an Executive Director encourage positive relationships and establish a healthy culture among staff and volunteers?

119

- What are ways to build leadership and management skills among paid and unpaid staff?
- How does an Executive Director build a culture of respect and trust for all staff?
- What are strategies for establishing strong lines of communication with staff?
- How can e-mail be used as an effective communication tool with staff?
- How does an Executive Director offer and receive support from staff and volunteers while keeping an arm's-length relationship?

How does an Executive Director who is new to an organization build quick credibility with paid and unpaid staff?

When you are hired as Executive Director of a nonprofit you are usually received with great expectations for success. The first few weeks as ED are the formative ones, and one of your goals should be to create an atmosphere of mutual trust and respect with your paid and unpaid staff. This is also the time when Executive Directors make their leadership and management styles known, and test them within the existing culture. Every ED brings a unique management and leadership style to the job. Being candid about this in the early days of working in the organization helps others develop understanding and trust.

Wisdom

The Executive Director plays many roles in working with staff and volunteers— manager, leader, mentor, coach, team player, and supporter.

There are many ways to get off to a good start with your staff and crystallize your personal style. However, we encourage all new Executive Directors to meet with each key paid and unpaid staff member within the first few days of beginning work to ask the following questions:

1. Do you feel you are effective in your current position? If not, is there some way I can support you to become more effective?

2. What are you expecting from me as the Executive Director? How can I best support you in your job?

3. In what ways would you like to develop yourself in your job?

4. What excites you about working here?

5. What barriers to getting your job done do you experience?

6. What is your preferred method of communication—e-mail, staff meetings, memos, phone calls, casual drop-ins?

7. How do you prefer to receive feedback?

The second question provides a natural opening for you to describe your expectations of them as a staff member. If you've clearly heard what they expect from you, it will be natural for them to listen to you in return. The seventh question provides a similar opportunity to discuss your own preferences for receiving feedback—and to emphasize that you want and need feedback from your staff. At the conclusion of the conversation, talk frankly about your roles as leader, manager, and supporter, and how you work with staff in these roles. This helps staff see that you see yourself adapting to various situations, and that you intend to be flexible depending on the circumstances.

Some organizations have a paid Executive Director with all other work being done by unpaid staff (generally called volunteers). Others have unpaid staff providing important support functions that assist those who are paid. Identifying who is key in these organizations is not just a matter of determining who has a position comparable to management, it requires finding out who the leaders are throughout the organization. Ask your staff who they go to when they want help, or need information, or just want to discuss something. The names that pop up repeatedly are probably people you want to meet with. They may or may not be in supervisory positions.

Once you have met with key staff people, you might set up a group meeting with remaining staff and jointly address some of the questions listed for the individual staff meetings, particularly those on expectations, job satisfaction, and job frustration. As Executive Director, you'll find it useful to know what motivates and what challenges your staff, as well as what they expect of you and what they need from you in order to get their jobs done smoothly. By taking time for these initial conversations, you show you are interested in those who work there, which helps create an environment of partnership and establish a foundation of trust.

In a very large organization—say, with upwards of a hundred paid and unpaid staff—you probably can't meet individually with each person. Instead, you could meet individually with the first two layers of management in traditionally structured organizations, or with team leaders in a team-structured organization. Then, follow up with group meetings for the remaining staff. It is important to determine what is going to work best in your particular organizational culture. There is no one way to learn more about those who work in the nonprofit. The crucial point is to take the time to do so.

These meetings are just the beginning of building credibility with staff. Periodic follow-up is essential. One way to build a healthy environment is to establish a "values statement" with staff—a document that spells out expectations of how people will work together in partnership. This serves as the foundation for your ongoing relationships with everyone. The list in Exhibit 11.1 gives you some ideas on what you might want to have in a values statement.

If you can jointly develop a values statement with staff, then you more readily assure your credibility. When people in an organization trust and respect the Executive Director, a healthy, productive environment is the result, and the Executive Director is less likely to experience that "lonely at the top" syndrome that is so prevalent in the position.

Wisdom

Take time to view the organization through the eyes of your staff and understand their accomplishments, needs, and expectations of your role.

Exhibit 11.1 Key Elements of a Staff Values Statement

We will keep commitments we make. If we cannot keep a commitment, we will explain why.

We will stay focused on priorities and be accountable for agreed-upon outcomes and deadlines.

We will follow through on every assignment we accept. If we cannot meet a deadline for a task, we will give sufficient notice and explain why.

We will give and receive constructive and honest feedback on work-related matters.

We will openly acknowledge mistakes and errors and make efforts to learn from them.

We will seek input on decisions from those people who will be affected by the decisions.

We will work as a team to support each other and be ever conscious of the organization's mission and priorities in relationship to our own.

When your staff believes in you and respects you, they support your decisions and work with you to meet the goals of the organization.

How does an Executive Director encourage positive relationships and establish a healthy culture among staff and volunteers?

As the answer to an earlier question implies, the Executive Director serves as a role model for staff and in building positive relationships. This is just the beginning to creating a healthy culture for all.

Max De Pree, in *Leading Without Power*, describes the essentials of a vital organization. He explains that vital organizations exude health, energy, and enthusiasm. In other words, they have a culture that is robust, where people are working together productively to further the mission of the nonprofit and build its potential.

To paraphrase Max De Pree, some of the essentials that produce and maintain positive relationships among staff and volunteers are nourishment, justice, respect, confidence, and accountability. In the following list, we provide our translations of these powerful concepts. You can use these ideas to think about what is in place in your organization, and what you need to strengthen.

- *Nourishment:* An environment where people are constantly learning through taking on new tasks and participating in professional development activities, and are able to learn from making mistakes because they do not fear punishment.
- *Justice:* A culture that treats all staff and volunteers equally and fairly in terms of compensation, workload, and opportunities for promotion.
- *Respect:* An environment where staff and volunteers know their voices are heard and valued, and where good manners prevail.
- *Confidence:* Every person in the organization believes that they and those served by the nonprofit will enjoy a brighter future, and that their commitment to their cause is making a significant difference in society.
- *Accountability:* A culture where all staff and volunteers know what is expected of them and are recognized and rewarded for their good work.

When these essentials are in place, relationships are more likely to be strong and the people active in the nonprofit to be working productively. It is also important for you, as Executive Director, to know that creating positive relationships and a healthy culture are not your job alone. *It is everyone's job to create a healthy culture.* If few of these essentials are in place, you may need to encourage and support managers to develop new practices. Mentoring them is one way to provide support, as is supporting professional development that develops communication and relationship-building skills.

What are ways to build leadership and management skills among paid and unpaid staff?

To be successful in the caretaking role of Executive Director, you must encourage and develop leaders and managers in your nonprofit. Unless you keep the job for an unusually long time, these are the people who will stay after your departure and sustain the organization over the long haul.

As a leader and a manager, the Executive Director should serve as a role model for staff who are in these positions, or who may be interested in taking them on. The supporter role is also an important one for Executive Directors to take in developing managers and leaders. Providing encouragement, resources, and coaching to persons motivated to grow in their positions and take on more responsibility and authority is essential to this supporter role.

Here are some ways an Executive Director can develop management and leadership skills among the staff:

- Hire people who have the skills, or the potential to develop the skills, as leaders and managers.
- Understand that creating and nurturing leaders and managers in the organization is in no way a threat to the Executive Director's position. Instead, having others who lead and manage makes this position more doable.
- Encourage staff who are in management positions or who demonstrate leadership qualities to get more training and increase their skills in these areas so they are continually developing themselves.
- Empower staff to make their own decisions, or at least to suggest options and help select the best one, so as to build confidence among current and potential managers.
- Allow staff to make mistakes and turn them into learning experiences. It is far better to have a discussion on what could

have worked better, and what was learned from the mistake, than to spend time and energy on warnings, reprimands, or demotions.

This last point might make some Executive Directors uncomfortable, because it suggests that mistakes are okay to make. In general, this is true: everybody makes them, and if you banish everyone who ever made a mistake you won't have an occupied office in the organization, including your own. It's worth restating: build on mistakes, don't let them tear things apart. But draw the line at actions that intentionally harm the organization—they do need to be handled swiftly and will require some form of reprimand or dismissal.

It is important for Executive Directors to encourage staff to grow into their own management and leadership styles. Staff should be supported to develop themselves professionally, given tasks that challenge them (but not overly so), and allowed to take risks that don't jeopardize the organization. This allows them to develop on the job and become confident in their own levels of expertise.

How does an Executive Director build a culture of respect and trust for all staff?

Having a healthy culture for staff requires everyone to work hard toward this goal. An Executive Director cannot expect to make much headway in an organization where staff members are content with their negative environment.

Occasionally, a newly hired Executive Director walks into a culture that is lacking in trust and respect among staff. Because of this unhealthy culture, the Executive Director is immediately targeted as someone who should not be trusted or respected. If things blow up in your face before you've had a chance to do anything to set them off, it is very important to understand that the situation is not personal to you—it has probably been in place for some time. Any culture where you find people spending more time complaining about, blaming, and shaming each other than being productive is a culture that needs to be changed. It is generally the job of the Executive Director to take the lead.

For instance, if you find that staff have fallen into a habitual trap of negativity, resisting feedback, fighting new ideas, feeding unproductive rumor mills, and spending significant time talking about one another in negative tones, it's likely that they will almost immediately voice concerns about you as well. In that case, it's important to start changing this slowly by asking people to talk about their working environment and the overall culture of the nonprofit. Invite everyone to openly discuss what they like about working at the nonprofit, what originally brought them to it, what is frustrating, what is needed to create a more harmonious environment, and other such questions.

While you will probably notice resistance, we think you will also get some very good information to help shape a new culture. Also, if you are genuinely interested in the feedback you are receiving and demonstrate your interest, trust begins to build for you and your position. Talk to staff about what you are finding and how the culture is not a productive or healthy one for anyone working there, and work with them to make changes toward a more positive environment. Some of the exercises in Chapter Four, on nonprofit culture, may be useful here.

Quickly identifying cultural issues and explaining them to everyone helps staff see the Executive Director as someone who can be objective. Quickly making changes to create a more positive culture helps everyone see that you are interested in their having a positive work experience.

Story from the Field

A recently hired Executive Director learned within three weeks of starting her job at an environmental organization that her seven-member staff group was very dissatisfied with the organization and did not trust that the Board had made a good decision in hiring her. Rather than taking this somewhat blatantly stated reaction personally, she moved quickly to set up meetings with each staff person and with her five-member Board. She suspected that there were tensions between Board members and staff and she guessed correctly. Through her meetings with everyone, she learned that the previous Executive Director had created a culture where threats and intimidation were the norm, people were encouraged to work separately and in competition for resources, and to believe that if something was wrong, it was the Board's fault. Nobody was very happy and the Board Chair finally explained to her that she was hired because they thought she could fix things.

Eventually this Executive Director did create a new culture of mutual respect and trust. It took more than a year, and a few people who enjoyed the status quo chose to leave. She started to make the change by being clear about what she learned in her meetings with everyone and by explaining how this type of unhealthy culture was hurting the nonprofit, which meant it was also hurting the people being served. She formed a joint Board-staff task force to work with her on short-term and longer-term strategies to build trust and engage everyone in fulfilling the mission together.

What are strategies for establishing strong lines of communication with staff?

The focus on one-on-one conversations with staff and establishing a values statement mentioned earlier are two strategies that open up good lines of communication. Some other strategies are useful to consider as well.

WARNING

Never isolate yourself from your staff through a lack of communication or involvement.

Good communication involves understanding that you need to communicate effectively throughout all levels of your nonprofit. Too many Executive Directors discuss important issues with their management team, and then let them pass the information on to others. Inevitably the information gets reworded as it moves through the organization, and the intended message becomes distorted or even lost. It's like Post Office—the game children play of whispering something in someone's ear, who then whispers it in the next person's ear, and on down the line to the last person, who has to say what the first person originally whispered. The person at the end of the line always says something radically different from what the first person said!

If you have something important to say to your staff and volunteers, say it to everyone. Using this approach allows you to immediately answer questions, dispel fears and rumors, and show people you genuinely respect them. In turn, they will most likely respect and support you.

While providing good information to staff is important, perhaps the greatest gift of all to everyone is your ability to listen well. We encourage all Executive Directors to spend time every day just listening to staff in the organization, and being clear that every voice in the nonprofit is important.

Here are some other strategies to encourage good communication in your nonprofit:

- Use a variety of techniques to communicate. Some people take in information by reading it, others want to hear it.

- Encourage people to listen and to hold real dialogs with one another.

- Be clear about who needs to know what. While everyone should know about decisions, events, changes, and other happenings at the nonprofit, not everyone needs to know every detail. You want to include a high level of detail for people who are affected directly by the information or who may need to give explanations to others outside the organization. Others just need to know that something new has taken place.

- Encourage feedback. Find ways to make it easy for staff and volunteers to make suggestions for improvement, such as a suggestion box or special meetings with you to just brainstorm new ways of working at your organization. Create an evaluation system that involves input from a variety of people close to the person being evaluated. This representative feedback system from all levels of the organization provides specific feedback against specific goals. Rather than ask everyone in the organization to participate, the staff person being evaluated identifies three to five people and the supervisor identifies three to five people to provide input.

- Practice self-management when someone criticizes or disagrees with you. Remember it is that person's perspective, and work together to determine what is at the source of the critical view or perspective.

- Create a zero-tolerance environment for staff and volunteers who come to you with complaints about others and have not tried to work out their complaints with the individuals involved. As Executive Director, you should support effective conflict resolution between staff and volunteers—not step in and do it yourself and deprive them of the opportunity. The first step is to have individuals talk to each other about problems they have with one another. Offer suggestions, role-play ways to work out conflicts, mediate if you need to, but don't ever take matters into your own hands until those in conflict have tried to work out their differences.

How can e-mail be used as an effective communication tool with staff?

As nonprofits become more and more savvy about computers and technology, we see much more reliance on e-mail as a communication strategy. This is both good and bad. E-mail is great for getting those quick announcements out to people, to tell them about visitors coming to the organization, new grant money received, upcoming staff meetings, and the like.

Where e-mail fails miserably is in communicating anything that evokes divergent viewpoints that need to be expressed and discussed. For instance, Mim worked for a while with an Executive Director who communicated everything by e-mail. He recognized individuals for their good work via e-mail. He offered constructive criticism via e-mail. He gave notice of his decisions to everyone using e-mail. He essentially communicated exclusively via e-mail. When asked why, he explained that it saved an enormous amount of time to send out an e-mail message, rather than hunt around for an individual or call a meeting. That was true enough, but what he failed to recognize was that his communication was all one-way, leaving staff feeling remote, cut off, and with little input or connection. The organization was suffering in terms of both communication with and respect for the Executive Director.

Wisdom

A healthy organizational culture is built upon an environment of mutual respect and shared values.

How does an Executive Director offer and receive support from staff and volunteers while keeping an arm's-length relationship?

The implication in this question is that there must be an arm's-length relationship rather than friendship or anything more intimate between the Executive Director and staff. We agree with this basic premise; leading and managing friends or loved ones is a tricky and very difficult job for an Executive Director. Boundaries become fuzzy, resentment builds, and the Executive Director's credibility can fade.

Warning

Never have an intimate relationship with another staff member.

This does not mean that an Executive Director should not have personal interactions with staff. As a matter of fact, we encourage some level of personal interaction as a way to build a strong staff team. Executive Directors all need to create their own boundaries regarding these personal interactions. The following guidelines may help in establishing such boundaries:

- Keep your very personal (intimate) life outside the organization. If you are having problems with a loved one, leave those at home.
- Be open about your interests, food cravings, and favorite things to do.
- If anyone on the staff tries to get you to serve as therapist, help them move their attention to a trained professional in this field. (And if you are one, help them find someone else.)
- If you find a friendship developing with a staff person, be clear that your primary responsibility in the friendship is to the nonprofit where you both work, and the friendship will always come second.
- Never, ever engage in an intimate relationship with one of your staff (paid or unpaid).

This does not mean that Executive Directors should not seek out staff or volunteers for support. You can and should turn to trusted individuals in your organization, people whose opinions you value, for the purpose of bouncing ideas off them, getting needed input before making decisions, or just having some fun. Just draw the line—and never cross it—at seeking out staff to vent frustrations, talk about other staff or board members, or complain about how miserable life is at that moment. These are topics that are better handled outside the organizations with friends, family, a coach, or anyone who is not directly involved in the organization.

CHAPTER TWELVE

Following the Founder

Founder's Syndrome occurs when an organization operates according to the personality of the most prominent person in the organization rather than working toward its overall mission. This prominent person may be the Founder, Board Chair or Executive Director. The syndrome is primarily an organizational issue, not simply the fault of the person of prominence.

—CARTER MCNAMARA

ORGANIZATIONS ARE USUALLY STARTED by someone with an incredible vision and strong passion to address a pressing need or to initiate change. In the early days of an organization, the Founder keeps the vision alive with personal energy, passion, gutsiness, and quite often financial resources as well.

While the term *Founder* originally referred to the person who began an organization, it has since been expanded to apply to anyone with long-term prominence and authority in an organization, such as the first Executive Director or anyone whose identity has become tied so closely to the organization that they are seen *as* the organization.

Just as moving through adolescence with a child is frequently a highly emotional time, so too we find that a mix of emotions emerges as Founders watch their nonprofits grow up. There is joy for the success of the nonprofit. There is sadness for leaving the good old days. And often, there is some fear of letting go of the attention that being the focal point for the organization has afforded the Founder.

Releasing the responsibilities seems to be the easier part. Giving up authority, visibility, and leadership of the organization is more challenging—not only for the Founder but also for others in the organization who will have to change their comfortable ways of doing things.

This chapter will address the following issues that typically arise for a new Executive Director dealing with a Founder who still wants to be engaged in a nonprofit:

- Why do relationships with Founders in transition tend to be so complicated?
- What is the best way for an Executive Director to work with a Founder who is still a member of the Board of Directors?
- What does the Executive Director do if the Founder is causing serious problems for the organization?
- What are the pros and cons of having the Founder stay on as a staff person or consultant?

Why do relationships with Founders in transition tend to be so complicated?

Eventually, the Founder discovers that the nonprofit is taking on a life of its own. This usually happens when the Board has grown beyond being just the friends of the Founder, or when the first Executive Director (beyond the Founder) is hired, or when a funder has taken a special interest in the organization and has significantly increased funding for programs, which then intensifies subsequent demands for accountability.

In organizational life cycle terms, the nonprofit finds it must grow from its start-up, entrepreneurial roots into a well-managed organization with systems, policies, and planning. Board members must move beyond their mostly reactive engagement with the Founder's individual style toward a more proactive, consensus-oriented model of decision making. In other words, the organization experiences a major cultural shift.

Organizational culture emerges to become more visible and critical during periods of Founder transition. Before successors can begin to understand or adapt the culture toward their own personal leadership style, they must understand its roots, the factors that led to its development, and how this all influences the organization's thoughts and actions.

When an organization hires its first Executive Director to step into the activities once done by a Founder, tensions related to the Founder's process of letting go—as well as that of the rest of the organization—often emerge. They need to be addressed early in this new developing relationship. The incoming Executive Director wonders what to do with this amazing person who started the nonprofit and poured years of life into it. The staff and Board are sometimes torn between their allegiance to the Founder and to the newly hired ED whose success they hope for. The Founder grapples with the desire to delegate day-to-day responsibilities in the face of continuing passion and love of the visibility and authority of the Founder identity.

Shifts in a Founder's role and authority ripple throughout the entire organization, and sometimes into the external community as well. The visibility and strength that the Founder brings to the organization start to become a hindrance as individuals—and sometimes the Founder as well—have trouble letting go of the old ways.

What is the best way for an Executive Director to work with a Founder who is still a member of the Board of Directors?

The Founder as Board member works well if that person understands that the position carries the same responsibilities as that of other Board members and an equal voice—no more and no less. This is a big if.

Usually the transition from a Founder-driven Board to a Board led by a strong Executive Director is challenging. More and more organizations allow, suggest, or request that their Founder take a well-deserved break for a year or so. This allows the Founder's vision and work to evolve under the new ED's leadership.

Suppose you are the first Executive Director of a nonprofit where the Founder has always worn the hats of Board member, Board Chair, and Executive Director. On one hand you see the opportunity to work with someone who has incredible passion for the nonprofit. On the other hand, you may notice that the Founder has a tendency to micromanage your work to ensure that everything continues as it should—at least in the Founder's eyes. Building a trusting relationship with the Founder necessitates constant communication, reassurance, and some frank discussions about your ED role relative to the Founder's new role. As new staff members (paid and unpaid) are added to the organization, you may also need to hold meetings with the full Board to further define the changing roles of the Founder, the Executive Director, and others.

A Founder often retains a Board position but frequently chooses not to be a key officer. This can be tricky to manage. On one hand, the Founder wants others to take on leadership roles. However, when disagreeing with a decision, the Founder may quite actively struggle to take the reins away from the new leaders. When this happens, the Board Chair must step in to gently remind the Founder that Board members can legitimately disagree on issues, but when a decision is made, it is a Board decision and all must accept it.

It can be very helpful for everyone to define a particular Board task for a Founder that channels all that passion and energy in a valuable direction. For example, we have seen Founders asked to develop a written history of the organization and to periodically provide stories to Board members to help everyone understand an organization's roots. We have also seen Founders become major fundraisers because of their charisma and energy.

Another Board member role for the Founder is as an emeritus. Emeritus status elevates Founders to honorary membership on the Board, allowing them to attend meetings whenever interested and give wise advice when asked. An emeritus Board member often does not have voting rights but is able to have a voice at the table whenever needed or desired.

What does the Executive Director do if the Founder is causing serious problems for the organization?

In our years of working with nonprofits we have encountered a few situations where the Founder was seriously hindering the progress and success of an organization. A clear indicator of such a circumstance is that everyone in the nonprofit is unhappy most of the time—including the Founder, who often does not understand the source of the problems.

If you as Executive Director find yourself facing this dilemma, proceed with caution and allow the mission rather than the personalities to be your guide. First, make sure you are not projecting your misery with the Founder onto everyone else. In other words, see if the Board and other staff members are seeing the issues in the same light. Often they share your concern that the Founder is creating problems for the organization but don't know how to initiate the conversation, let alone resolve it. Work with the Board to help its members take the initiative and lead the process. Gather concrete examples of what the Founder is doing that is harmful. Then, have the Board Chair or Executive Committee meet with you and the Founder to discuss the problems openly and candidly.

Wisdom

Take time to get to know and understand your Founder's vision, passion, and gifts. Honor and respect the Founder's contributions, recognize and talk about the challenges of letting go, and discuss how that affects your new responsibilities and authority.

It is very important that the conversation with the Founder be conducted with compassion and respect. This is not a discussion to have when hot tempers are fully engaged. Remember, and make reference to, all the wonderful work the Founder has done. Reinforce for everyone the common vision and passion for the organization that you all share. Then describe very specifically and concretely the actions of the Founder that are hurting the organization. If you describe these actions in the context of the nonprofit growing to a new level where success requires meeting new and different needs, rather than putting the Founder's efforts down, you and the Board stand a better chance of making your point effectively.

Expect anger, tears, silence, denial, and a wide range of other unhappy emotions. Remember too that when emotions are allowed expression in an atmosphere of respect and compassion, energy is often freed up and everyone can more easily share new perspectives. This is the nature of difficult conversations. If the Founder is truly hampering an organization, not having this conversation is more than likely to prolong the unhealthy behaviors that can eventually damage both the Founder and the organization's reputation.

Wisdom

Founders can be an ongoing asset to an organization in either a volunteer, board, or staff role with clearly defined roles, lines of communication, and authority that doesn't compete with that of the Executive Director.

There may be room for negotiation in this meeting. If the issue is one of divided loyalty, staff and stakeholders need to have their support redirected toward the organization so they're no longer torn between allegiances to either the Founder or ED. Perhaps the Founder can take on a goodwill ambassador role outside the nonprofit. Don't close the door on the possibility of an ongoing relationship. But if it is clear that there is no possibility for such a relationship, then your Board or Executive Committee members should gently but firmly let the Founder know that the nonprofit no longer has a role for the Founder to assume.

What are the pros and cons of having the Founder stay on as a staff person or consultant?

When a nonprofit is making the transition from an all-volunteer group in which the Founder has taken the responsibilities of both Chair and ED to hiring its first paid Executive Director, the Founder sometimes chooses to take the paid position. There are many pros to this move. The Founder knows the organization and everyone knows the Founder. Often the Founder *is* the nonprofit and that transfers to the new position very smoothly. Basically, the programs or services of the organization proceed without disruption and this is a major plus. Having the incredible vision, passion, and energy of the Founder leading the organization on a daily basis is of course an extraordinary benefit.

But having the Founder become the first paid ED does bring some challenges. It is complex to define and set boundaries between the leadership roles of the Executive Director, the Founder, and the Board.

WARNING

As challenges arise, never denigrate the individual; instead focus on the symptoms and issues. Remember that Founder's Syndrome is primarily an organizational problem.

Story from the Field

Mim was recently in a Board meeting where the Executive Director, who is the Founder and who had formerly been the Board Chair, was running the meeting and making decisions while Board members simply nodded their heads in agreement. Presented with the rationale for separation of authority between Board Chair and Executive Director, everyone thought this was a good idea and agreed to move forward quickly to strengthen the Chair's authority and leadership role. It looked like the group would move into its next stage smoothly, but Mim found out later that the Founder continued to make all the decisions, and the partnership between the Board and the ED-Founder was clearly deteriorating as resentment grew among Board members.

To better understand the friction, Mim met with Board members individually and asked questions regarding each person's ideas for a better partnership. Then Mim met with the Founder to explain what she had heard and to relay how the Founder's need to control the organization was actually harmful. Of course, the Founder had no idea that the rest of the Board was upset, and agreed something should be done to correct the situation.

The Executive Committee met with the Founder and began the slow process of transition from Founder-led to a stronger Board-ED partnership.

New roles and responsibilities were defined as well as clear lines of authority for decisions. Board members discussed their interests and skills and began taking on some of the tasks the Founder had originally done. All these changes led to a much better partnership, and to a healthier culture for this nonprofit.

If you are an Executive Director who founded your organization and also used to be the Board Chair, watch out for the natural tendency to keep both roles. Take time to determine if you are building a healthy relationship with your Chair and Board members.

Sometimes a Founder will want to remain in a staff position in the organization, but not as the Executive Director. One of the pros to this is the knowledge the Founder brings to the organization. Another is that Founders who make this choice usually want a staff role congruent with their gifts and skills, thus eliminating the potential to fill the position with an unqualified individual.

The most important potential con to hiring the Founder in a staff role lies in the sheer difficulty of stepping out of a position of authority, working in partnership with someone who now holds that authority, and reporting to the Board through new lines of communication. A truly greathearted Founder can do this, especially if the environment stays reasonably consistent for a few years after the transition. If things don't work out, however, the new Executive Director is in an almost untenable position. Imagine yourself with a Founder on staff who disagrees with your vision and leadership of the organization. The Founder can do some serious damage to your credibility by going to friendly Board members and making disparaging remarks about you. While these might be grounds for termination from a strict personnel management viewpoint, can you do this if the Board is supporting the Founder's position?

It is this scenario—which has repeated itself countless times in our experience—that leads us to the conclusion that Founders should not

WARNING

Don't confront the Founder on your own; instead, work with and through the Board to resolve issues with the Founder.

be hired as staff, other than as the Executive Director. The risk of harming the progress and success of the organization is too great.

Founders can and should be engaged as consultants—in their area of expertise. The obvious benefit is that you get a consultant who already knows your organization well and has a lot of loyalty to your mission. Also, as the client to the Founder-consultant, you set the project parameters and define the criteria for success. Since projects are time limited, the Founder-consultant can do a specific job and then move on to something else.

No matter what position the Founder takes in your organization, the responsibilities have to be very clear so the Founder fully understands and accepts the new role. Boundaries on decision making (what decisions the Founder can make now) and clarity on what you hold the Founder accountable for should also be stated up front. Remember also that the more specific the project for a Founder, the more likely that person will be successful, and the more likely there will be a good relationship between the Executive Director and Founder.

WARNING

Everything can look perfectly smooth until the day the Founder disagrees with something the Executive Director regards as necessary.

PART FIVE

Executive Director as Community Creator

The leaders of all institutions will have to learn that it is not enough for them to lead their own institutions . . . they will also have to learn to become leaders in the community. In fact, they will have to learn to create community.

—PETER DRUCKER

NONPROFIT ORGANIZATIONS and their leaders increasingly play a dual role, furthering their own mission by working collaboratively with other organizations and within their own communities. These collaborative approaches are built on mutual benefit, and they reward the individuals involved, their nonprofit organizations, and the broader community. Thus the term *community creator*.

This section of the book examines relationship building beyond the walls of the organization. Chapter Thirteen explores the rewards of informal relationships with a variety of stakeholders, and Chapter Fourteen focuses on more long-term, strategic partnerships such as collaboration and strategic alliances. Chapter Fifteen support EDs in building organizations that reflect the diversity of the communities they serve.

CHAPTER THIRTEEN

Engaging External Stakeholders

You cannot build relationships without having an understanding of your potential partners, and you cannot achieve that understanding without a special form of communication that goes beyond ordinary conversation. In other words, you need to engage in dialogue.
—DANIEL YANKELOVICH, *The Magic of Dialogue*

NONPROFITS THRIVE when they have a committed group of external stakeholders ready to provide support through advocacy, funding, and furthering the mission. These stakeholders give added passion and commitment to your cause and create a strong voice in the community. Generally, the more external stakeholders an organization has, the more influence and visibility it has in serving and advocating on behalf of those in need. At the same time, the more visible an organization is through its marketing and public relations, the easier it is to attract new stakeholders.

W̶isdom

Dare to venture beyond your organization's walls and reach out to a variety of stakeholders who can or should have an interest in your organization.

The term *stakeholders* is widely used in our nonprofit vocabulary, yet many outside the sector are caught off-guard by its common reference and broad use. In the non-profit sector, the term has come to define any individual or group that has, or should have, an interest or stake in your organization's mission

145

and accomplishments. Although businesses typically define *stakeholders* narrowly as direct customers and investors, nonprofits regard a complex matrix of individuals and groups who bring a broad range of resources as well as expectations as legitimate stakeholders in their affairs.

In addition to being a source of visibility and resources for nonprofits and support for the executive director, stakeholders can present challenges and barriers when they are overlooked or misunderstood. Thus we have dedicated a chapter to helping you answer the following questions:

- Who are an organization's external stakeholders?
- How can the Executive Director develop and nurture relationships with key stakeholders?

Who are an organization's external stakeholders?

Preceding chapters have discussed four of the most visible internal stakeholders in any nonprofit: the Board, staff, volunteers (or unpaid staff), and the Founder. But the discussion can't stop there. You also need to look beyond the organization's walls for ideas, insights, trends, and needs in your community. Every organization should be asking itself who the individuals and groups are that it should be nurturing or exploring. We encourage you to do this by taking time as part of your strategic planning process or annual goal-setting to evaluate the importance of identifying stakeholders who may be critical to helping you reach your stated goals, as well as those who might hinder your work.

We have found that most nonprofit organizations have two general groups of external stakeholders. The first group is often very obvious to everyone because they touch your organization on a regular basis. The second group can be easy to overlook without some forethought of how they connect with your nonprofit, or should connect.

Your First Priorities

- Your clients or customers
- Prospective clients or customers
- Families of clients or customers
- Individual major donors
- Foundation and corporate funders
- Government funders
- Prospective funders
- Regulatory agencies
- Vendors you contract with or buy from

Sometimes Overlooked

- Community leaders
- Local, regional, and national politicians and their staff
- Neighbors near your facilities or offices
- Your landlord or property owner
- Former Board members or advisory boards
- Former clients, staff, and volunteers
- Nonprofit organizations with similar or competing programs
- Businesses with complementary or competing programs
- The media
- Companies whose employees benefit from your mission or services
- Nonprofit management support organizations

WARNING

Stakeholders who are overlooked or misunderstood can be a source of negative public relations and hinder your organization's work.

This list should help you in developing your own targeted list of individuals or groups that you already have a relationship with but need to nurture, and those where new relationships may be critical to your organization's mission or future plans.

How can the Executive Director develop and nurture relationships with key stakeholders?

Getting the word out about the needs in your community and how your nonprofit is responding to those needs is important to your success in achieving your vision and fulfilling your mission. One great way to get the word out is to be accessible to the media, government officials, and opinion leaders who are interested in and sensitive to your mission. They can be excellent resources or spokespersons. Current and future external stakeholders need constant reminders of your organization's accomplishments, and of your values and purpose. This builds commitment to your mission and creates a small army of dedicated individuals.

Day-to-day demands often take up so much attention that an Executive Director becomes isolated from the rest of the world. It takes planning and initiative to reach beyond the boundaries of your organization to be reminded of the bigger community perspective and your broader civic responsibility.

The key to building and maintaining any relationship is dialog and understanding what is important to the other party. For example, you probably already have communications tools in place for your clients that describe or market your programs. But do you really know who your customers are, where they come from, and what they value about your services? Your donors send you a check and you respond with an acknowledgment or thank you. But do you know why they give to you or their connection with your mission?

Wisdom

Relationships are built on communication. Effective communication starts with listening.

What these questions point to is that the underlying principle of working with stakeholders is to develop a healthy pattern of two-way communication. The first step is to listen—get to know them, their current or potential interest in your organization, what they expect of you and your organization, and how they subjectively or objectively evaluate the outcomes or satisfaction. The second step is to educate, inform, and ask for their feedback, insight, and support.

While a face-to-face meeting is often the most effective way to engage in dialog, it isn't a very efficient form of communication when you have large groups of stakeholders. The communication ladder illustrated in Exhibit 13.1 has been adapted over the years as the Internet has grown. It lists the various forms of communication from the most effective to least effective way to engage in dialog (listen, inform, educate, and ask for feedback and support), and from the least efficient to most efficient ways to reach your target audience. Some may debate the effectiveness of e-mail versus "snail mail" for a personal letter depending on where you live, but the ladder does help you to think about the efficiency-effectiveness trade-off in identifying the most appropriate tools for your specific message to stakeholders.

As you develop your stakeholder strategy, make sure to include your Board and staff. Board members may

WARNING

Never take the case or perceived need for your programs and services for granted. You must ensure constant education and raise the visibility for your organization's mission, vision, and values.

Exhibit 13.1 Communication Ladder

Most Effective
Personalized
Message

Least Efficient
Tool to Reach
Stakeholders

1. One-on-one-communication
2. Personal phone call
3. Group discussion or focus group
4. Personal letter
5. Personal e-mail
6. Impersonal or group letter or e-mail
7. Newsletter or brochure
8. Web site
9. Media

Least Effective

Most Efficient

already have a relationship and credibility with a specific individual or group stakeholder. Funders and regulatory agencies may want to hear directly from key management in the programs or on the front lines.

Story from the Field

Following two years of troubled Board and staff leadership that had left it on the verge of financial crisis, a mental health organization hired a seasoned Executive Director from outside. The organization was presently at risk of losing critical government funding, referrals from other agencies, and licenses required by the state government to do its work.

Working with the Board and staff, the new ED helped the group develop the plan shown in Exhibit 13.2 as the first phase of a stakeholder strategy designed to rebuild the organization and its reputation. The plan outlined the use of various communication tools, prioritized the key stakeholders, and clarified what the nonprofit needed to learn (or listen to) as well as the key message it needed to deliver, along with the proposed support it was looking to gain and a plan of ongoing communication.

Exhibit 13.2 Stakeholder Communication Strategy

Stakeholder	Key Questions and Listening Points	Key Messages	Initial Communication Strategy	What Do They Value?	Follow-Up Communication
Ten largest major donors	What is your interest in us? What do you feel we are doing well? What could we improve upon? How do you feel we are perceived in the community?	We value your support. Share mission, vision, what is working, and turnaround strategy. Ask for specific gift to support turnaround.	Face-to-face meetings with ED and an appropriate Board member with existing relationship.	Accountability, ongoing communication, feeling that their funds are invested in a healthy organization.	Personal thank-you letter signed by ED and Board member, quarterly newsletter via mail or e-mail depending on preference.
Regulatory agencies	What are we doing well? What do we need to improve on? How much time do we have to reach compliance? What flexibility can they allow us? How we be evaluated? How can we rebuild our trust and partnership?	Acknowledge past problems. Ask for support and patience to get back on track. Share mission, vision, what is working, and turnaround strategy.	Face-to-face meeting with ED and key staff member.	Quantifiable results. Timely reports. No surprises.	Weekly or monthly updates on progress. Invitation to tour facility and programs in three months.
Former Board members	What is your current level of interest? How can you help?	We value your past support. Share mission, vision, what is working, and turn-around strategy.	Personal letter from Board Chair inviting them to call with feedback.	Being part of an organization they believe in and trust. Feeling valued.	Monthly e-mail updates on progress.

Exhibit 13.2 Stakeholder Communication Strategy (continued)

Stakeholder	Key Questions and Listening Points	Key Messages	Initial Communication Strategy	What Do They Value?	Follow-Up Communication
Staff	What attracted you to this job and the organization? What has been your greatest accomplishment? What is the greatest barrier to getting your job done? What one thing do you need to be more effective?	We value your dedication, skills, and views. We need your support to turn things around. Change is difficult. Share new strategy and reinforce the mission and vision.	Individual meetings between supervisors and ED. Group meeting with ED and Board member.	Being heard, included, and respected.	Ongoing personal, group, and written updates celebrating small successes and candor on the work that still needs to be done.
Clients	What are we doing well? Where can we improve? What is most important to you?	We value you as a customer. If necessary, apologize. We are listening and need your feedback. Remind them of mission and vision.	Small focus groups.	Our interest in their views. Willingness to work with them to implement suggestions.	Bulletin board in all facilities that updates clients. Quarterly newsletter.
Other nonprofit agencies that refer clients to us	What are we doing well? Where do we need to improve? How can we best partner to support each other? What are your expectations about how we will serve those you refer to us?	Thank you for your past support and referrals. We are committed to working with you and providing quality services to those you refer to us.	Face-to-face meeting with senior staff.	Quality programs. Partnership between organizations.	Monthly follow-up meetings to keep lines of communication open and explore joint problem solving.

Creating the plan is only the first step. Implementation of this kind of turnaround strategy requires

- A realistic but tight time frame
- Leadership and coordination from the ED, Board, and key management staff
- Individuals with the appropriate skills and connections
- A process to integrate responses and feedback so that the key messages are not lost
- Ongoing commitment to listen and communicate with stakeholders, updating them on the situation and accomplishments

Few organizations can accomplish their true potential by themselves. They need the support and wisdom of key individuals and groups that have or should have a stake in their mission. Take the time to look beyond your organization's walls for those who could be instrumental in helping you achieve your mission, as well as those that might present barriers.

CHAPTER FOURTEEN

Embracing Partnerships and Collaboration

No nonprofit organization can survive and succeed in advancing its mission while living independent of other nonprofits. Organizations gain information, political power, and personal and professional support from and in concert with other nonprofits. Thus close working relationships, partnerships and even joint ventures between nonprofit organizations are a fairly natural occurrence.

—DAVID LA PIANA, La Piana Associates, Inc.

A VARIETY OF PARTNERSHIPS from collaborations to mergers are evolving as extensions of an organization's relationships with its stakeholders. Nonprofit leaders are embracing the necessity of "leading beyond the walls" of each individual organization and developing partnerships that thrive on shared strengths and views. Many Executive Directors find that through short-term collaborations as well as formal structured strategic alliances they can better fulfill their mission, especially when faced with the breadth and complexity of the changing community needs and increasing competition for donor dollars.

The main difference between a stakeholder and partnership relationship is that in a partnership, such as a collaboration, two or more organizations have joined forces to publicly work toward some mutual benefit and have agreed to some distributed or shared power or authority. In contrast, stakeholder relationships are often casual, the benefits are assumed, and there is no shift in authority or power.

Nonprofits have several options when considering new ways to work more collaboratively with other organizations. Many excellent resources can help guide nonprofits through this organizational change. One of the contributors to the growing knowledge base on the subject for nonprofits is David La Piana. David brings much clarity to the whole field of nonprofit partnerships with his explanation of what he calls the "Partnership Continuum." The partnership continuum identifies a full range of options, from casual collaborative relationships that allow each organization a great deal of autonomy to the more fully integrated and permanent relationship formed by a merger, which integrates two or more organizations into one.

In this chapter we explore partnerships as an effective tool in helping nonprofits build their capacity and community. These are some of the questions that we address:

Wisdom

There are many forms of partnership to consider, starting at simple exchanges of information with stakeholders and ranging to fully integrated mergers.

- How can Executive Directors assess the values and risks of leading their organizations into partnerships?
- What forms of partnership exist beyond informal collaboration?
- How can Executive Directors prepare their organizations to enter into partnerships?

How can Executive Directors assess the values and risks of leading their organizations into partnerships?

Partnerships among nonprofits have intensified in the last decade. The primary driving factor for many of these has been the issues facing our communities—poverty, crime, education, environment, housing, health, to name a few. These issues cannot be tackled effectively by any single organization. In addition, pressures from funders and tough economic realities have driven many collaborations, joint ventures, and mergers.

Some of the most effective partnerships have been started by Executive Directors seeking new solutions to old problems, looking for ways to work smarter rather than harder, or desiring economies of scale. These partnerships start simply by an invitation to get together to explore the what-if or why-not issues that are often unspoken.

Through partnerships, a variety of nonprofits have pooled their talent and resources to solve problems, create innovative programs, or simply work in a new and more effective way that increases their own capacity to serve.

Partnerships benefit organizations, communities, and the people that have led them in many ways. Here are a few examples of how partnerships can help support individual, organizational, or community capacity building:

- New leadership, communication, and negotiation skills are developed among the Executive Directors or organizational representatives that make up the group.

- Visibility is increased for the organizations and their representatives as a result of working on a collaborative effort or in another form of partnership.

- New insights with regard to issues, trends, research, opportunities, and challenges emerge from the sharing of other people's perspectives.

- Opportunities to capitalize on the collective strengths of the partners and minimize individual risks or weaknesses often become apparent.

- Economies of scale achieved through collectively undertaking projects such as research, marketing, fundraising, program development, and advocacy benefit everyone.

- Expansion of capacity allows organizations to service more clients, provide more comprehensive services, or broaden the reach of their services.

While the rewards of reaching beyond your organization's traditional walls are many, there are also inherent barriers. Partnerships require a great deal of time and attention that can pull the ED and staff away from internal priorities. The greatest challenge of forming sustainable partnerships is that they can undermine the individuals and organizations they bring together. The following factors often lead to trouble:

- Lack of adequate resources (time, money, leadership) required to address issues or achieve desired goals.
- Egos, self-interests, and political agendas that block effective and candid discussions.
- Lack of shared purpose or expectations.
- Inability of the partners to clearly establish roles, rights, and responsibilities.
- Unwillingness of the partners or their respective organizations to reach consensus or compromise.
- An unfavorable political or social climate that may not support the collaborative process or outcome.

By listing these challenges, our intention is not to deter you but rather to increase your awareness and perhaps allow you to address such issues before problems arise and thus provide a greater chance of reaching your stated goals.

Story from the Field

Margaret has been privileged to work with a group of domestic violence agencies that had a common goal of building transitional housing for their clients. Through their shared vision and purpose they have successfully overcome a variety of challenges that could easily have resulted in the respective agencies parting ways.

The vision for transitional housing originated as a solo project for one of the agencies. As staff members moved on to leadership roles in neighboring agencies, the project followed them. It was never able to get off the ground until the political climate shifted in a way that raised the awareness of domestic violence and housing issues locally, lowering the competitive barriers that had traditionally isolated the agencies. As the vision became large and visible, the case for the project took on a life of its own. The project formally became a collaboration that was rewarded with early funding and support from private, community, and government sources.

This success meant more work for the Executive Directors who originally came together. Rather than succumb to the challenges of leading their respective agencies while supporting the growing demands of the collaborative, they recognized that additional resources and skills needed to come to the table. Additional agencies with housing experience were invited to join the collaborative. Fundraising support was also hired to help with a collective campaign.

As the number of players in the collaborative grew, so did need for coordination and compromise. Each agency took turns providing leadership to the partnership and the funding campaign. Support staff in each organization shared the load by taking on clearly defined roles and responsibilities. Policies, procedures, and rights were negotiated and adopted.

Despite the visibility and success of the collaborative, the EDs were still feeling pulled between their own organizational issues and those of the collaborative. Boards began to challenge the time that was going into the collaboration at the expense of their own organizations. Board members had lost sight of the vision and the benefits of transitional housing to their respective missions.

The initial reaction was that the collaboration's success necessitated converting it into a stand-alone nonprofit organization. While this would solve many of the ongoing internal struggles the collaborative faced, funders made it very clear that part of their motivation for support was the unique nature

Wisdom

The ultimate key to a successful partnership, collaboration, or merger is to keep the vision, mission, and community needs foremost in all discussions; otherwise turf issues will undermine even the best of intentions.

of the collaboration, the collective expertise, and the minimal overhead costs associated with the project. After some self-reflection, the EDs recognized the need to increase communication with and among their Boards. They formed an advisory group with representatives of each participating group's Board. The result was to broaden and secure each organization's continued stake in the project.

So far, the collaborative has raised over $14 million and built two innovative projects that provide housing to more than forty families; it now has a third project under consideration. Struggles and occasional setbacks still occur. But the vision, shared purpose, and visible success have allowed the group to accomplish much more than they could ever have envisioned individually.

Collaboration is an incredible tool for organizations to pool their talent and resources in search of a common vision. It takes work, compromise, and vision to overcome inevitable issues of self-interest that keep many groups from sustaining their partnership.

What forms of partnership exist beyond informal collaboration?

The challenge and opportunity facing many nonprofits is to look beyond informal collaborations to more long-term, formal, or sustainable partnerships that will further both groups' missions and provide a broader foundation upon which they can build their capacity to serve their communities.

WARNING

Developing and supporting effective partnerships can be demanding, but the potential rewards are great.

As stated earlier in the chapter, a variety of partnership opportunities are available to nonprofits. As illustrated in Exhibit 14.1, each varies in the degree of autonomy, integration, collaboration, and legal restructuring needed by the organizations involved.

Exhibit 14.1 Partnership Continuum

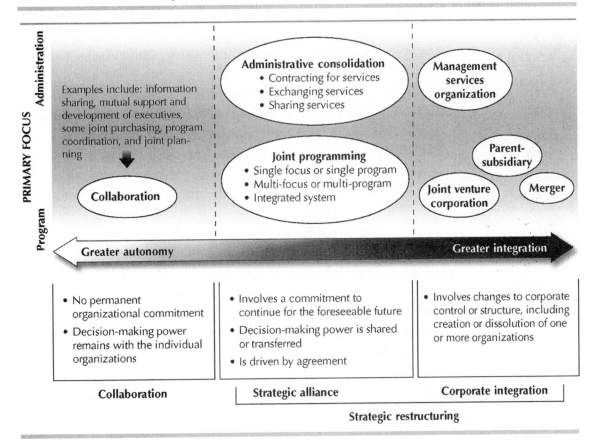

Source: David La Piana, *Nonprofit Mergers Handbook.*

The following list is a summary of the three most common ways nonprofits align their programs or integrate their organizations. In our experience many formal arrangements evolve out of highly successful collaborations. All of the following concepts fall into a category known as "strategic restructuring" because they involve a partial or total change in the structure and locus of control of the partners.

Joint Programming or *Joint Venture:* These are widely used terms that can mean anything from program collaboration between several nonprofits to activity that significantly alters a nonprofit's character. The terms are also applied to nonprofits with similar programs that decide to minimize competition by jointly conducting some activities, such as regional fundraising, marketing, or visibility campaigns.

For example, a joint fundraising venture among a group of nonprofits providing home-delivered meal services to local communities lessens competition for foundation grants and individual contributions and thus increases overall capacity to serve their communities. The Executive Directors of the meal delivery programs serve as the Board of Directors of a small subsidiary organization that has its own staff of two. The purpose of the subsidiary is to raise money for all the nonprofits involved, and over the years it has raised hundreds of thousands of dollars.

A new type of nonprofit/for-profit joint venture is emerging, as discussed in Chapter Seven. Corporate leaders are forming nonprofit extensions of their companies to support community philanthropy and initiatives. Nonprofits are forming for-profit services that funnel profits back into the nonprofit.

Administrative Consolidation: The sharing of core administrative functions, usually among nonprofits with similar missions and clients, characterizes a back-office consolidation. The organizations maintain their own Boards and staff and continue to exist as separate entities. However, some or all of their administrative functions are combined, such as payroll and human resource systems, financial and management information systems, and billing systems. There are lots of creative ways to make back-office consolidations work.

For example, suppose two organizations serving homeless individuals determine that, as single entities, they do not have the infrastructure to support program growth. Their administrative costs are soaring. If they combine their finance, human resources, and technology departments, significant advantages in efficiency and cost-effectiveness will result. The nonprofits continue to operate as separate entities, each with its own

ED and Board, but with a smoothly functioning, shared administrative department behind the scenes.

Merger: The legal and permanent blending of two or more nonprofits into a single entity is a merger. Rather than driven by the win-lose mentality or takeover approach common to corporate sector mergers, nonprofit mergers are usually driven by win-win opportunities to build on strengths and lessen risk.

Mergers are becoming a common restructuring practice and most communities have already experienced a merger between two nonprofits. Mergers are most successful when both parties agree to forfeit their current identity and establish an entirely new entity. Occasionally, the stronger partner in a nonprofit merger maintains its identity (either legally or symbolically), which results in a *consolidation* of the smaller nonprofit into the larger one. While consolidations are one good way to restructure, they are not true mergers.

Another term that is sometimes used for a restructuring is *acquisition.* In the nonprofit world, an acquisition is the same as a merger because nonprofit corporations cannot be bought or sold. Their assets must be transferred to a similar nonprofit organization under the close scrutiny of each state's Attorney General's office.

WARNING

Partnership requires a great deal of time and attention that can pull the ED, management staff, and Board away from internal priorities.

How can Executive Directors prepare their organizations to enter into partnerships?

Entering into any kind of partnership, be it marriage, new job, or collaboration, without first knowing your own strengths and expectations can be dangerous. Thus it makes sense to take time for self-reflection and assessment. What are your motivations for a specific partnership? Is this partner suitable? What are the strengths and weaknesses of your organization? What challenges and opportunities do you face?

Executive Directors need to ask themselves, their key staff, and their Board some key questions prior to undertaking a new venture. The following list is not exhaustive, but helps make explicit your motivations, fears, and potential benefits:

- What is driving our interest or desire to enter into this partnership?
- How will our mission be furthered by partnership?
- What do we specifically hope to gain from the partnership?
- What are we willing to contribute or share in terms of staff and Board time, expertise, or financial resources?
- Do Board, staff, and volunteers agree that a collaboration or partnership is beneficial?
- What is our history of working beyond our organization's boundaries?
- Do our potential partners share an environment of collaboration, trust, and mutual support?

If you are looking at a long-term strategic alliance or merger, you will want to explore many of the questions we raised regarding partnerships, as well as the following:

- Are we moving forward with restructuring because of desperation or fear, or do we really see advantages?
- What might we gain or lose in terms of our organizational identity and culture?
- Is the partnership being driven by a funder or external stakeholder? If so, what are implications to our commitment?

In response to the breadth and complexity of the changing nonprofit environment, nonprofits and business are exploring new ways of working together. Partnerships of all kinds are being formed to build capacity and better fulfill each group's mission.

CHAPTER FIFTEEN

Ensuring Broad Representation

The successful organization will review its policies, practices and organizational structure to remove potential barriers. . . . To truly value diversity means altering the power relations to minimize structural discrimination.

—DERALD WING SUE, *The Diversity Factor,* 1994, Vol. 2, No. 2

THE FABRIC OF SOCIETY is changing dramatically in terms of our ethnic, cultural, geographic, economic, religious, and other demographics. Nowhere is this more evident than in the population of the nonprofit sector—its clients, staff, volunteers, and external stakeholders.

The changing workforce in nonprofits means that organizations can expect broader representation in many areas—ethnicity, culture, age, religion, mental or physical ability, sexual preference, and political preferences, to name a few. To be successful, nonprofits will need to ensure their Boards and workforces reflect the communities they serve and are sensitive to differences in communication style, points of view, work style, and ways of managing conflict.

This chapter is designed to help Executive Directors promote an organizational culture that reflects the diversity of the community they serve and thrive in, as EDs alone cannot ensure broad representation in their nonprofit. The entire organization must openly embrace a culture of inclusion. As a matter of fact, it is not always appropriate for an Executive Director to be the strongest leader in this arena. As the answer to one of the questions in this chapter points out, an Executive Director must be aware of and able to successfully manage personal biases in order to be a strong and credible leader of a diverse organization. The Board, volunteers, and staff also need to participate in creating an atmosphere of understanding and work to eliminate their own biases.

The Executive Director should be watchful for others in the nonprofit who can share a leadership role in creating and sustaining a culture of broad representation. While the Executive Director must set the tone and lead by example, this is often a good place for the ED to follow others who have a deeper passion or greater resolve in this area.

With that in mind, here are the questions this chapter covers:

- What does *broad representation* mean for a nonprofit?
- How does an Executive Director lead an organization with broad and varied viewpoints, beliefs, and practices?
- Who holds the power in an organization and how are decisions made?
- How can an Executive Director be a positive role model in encouraging inclusion and diversity?
- How does an Executive Director manage diversity-related conflicts in an organization?

What does *broad representation* mean for a nonprofit?

Broad representation means that an organization is truly representative of the community it serves and is multicultural in the biggest sense of the word. It is conscious of diverse voices and experiences; it is fully accessible to the community it serves and is providing competent service to diverse populations; it goes beyond tolerating diversity to celebrate and honor differences.

Many people think that an organization is broadly representative if they can look around and see ethnic differences in those who work there, and among the Board or the clients served. But diversity is not simply an issue of race or ethnicity or visible disabilities, although these are important. Instead, it is the whole culture (values, policies, assumptions, practices, beliefs) that must be conscious and open to broad representation. And it is the Executive Director who must make sure this culture exists.

For an organization to be successful at obtaining and maintaining broad representation at all levels, the following must be in place:

Today's nonprofit organizations should strive for broad representation that goes far beyond the surface level of visible differences for staff, Board, and volunteers. The entire culture of the organization must honor diversity.

- The organization should reflect the contributions and interests of diverse cultures, religions, and ethnic, social, economic, geographic, and political groups in its mission, values, operations, and services.

- It should view the differences between people as a source of strength.

- It should be committed to precluding harassment in all forms within the organization.

- Decisions that shape the organization should be based on broad representation at all levels (Board, staff, volunteer, client) through the use of management practices and policies that emphasize participation and empowerment of people so they can perform to their full potential.

- The organizational culture should value people for what they *do* and who they *are.*

How does an Executive Director lead an organization with broad and varied viewpoints, beliefs, and practices?

To lead a diverse organization, the Executive Director and other staff, volunteers, and Board leaders should instill the values to sustain a multicultural consciousness. Some of these values are equity, inclusion, parity, and empowerment. When you read your values statement or organizational philosophy, do you see these values somewhere? If not, a broader discussion with Board members and staff is needed to ensure that the values are fully integrated in the organization, not just in materials for the public. It is very important that everyone understands and accepts these values and that they have a shared meaning in your organization.

The workplace environment is also a part of being culturally conscious. Ask yourself these questions:

- Do workplace signs, staff materials, and other written information meet the language needs of staff and people who are being served by them?
- Is the workplace fully accessible for persons with disabilities?
- Are holidays and vacation schedules sensitive to the religious and cultural needs of staff?
- Are the work processes of certain jobs adapted so that their essential functions can be successfully accomplished by individuals with disabilities?
- Do our policies address discrimination or harassment in the workplace?
- Do we have flexible work schedules to accommodate individuals who cannot work the traditional 9-to-5 day?
- What is our plan for ensuring that the Board has broad representation? Does it include practices that ensure inclusiveness and respect for differing opinions?

If you can answer yes at all points, then you are creating a healthy culture for broad representation. If not, then you and your Board leadership need to create it. A good place to start is with a task force of staff and Board members to identify a vision of your ideal multicultural workplace and a plan to achieve it. Then your leadership and that of others on the task force is needed to make sure that the plan is carried out and the vision is realized.

The Executive Director also needs to look at formal and informal relationships in the organization. Who talks to whom? In the halls, meetings, retreats, or other gatherings, do you see staff clustering based on their similarities, or is there a comfortable atmosphere where everyone interacts with everyone else regardless of differences?

Who holds the power in an organization and how are decisions made?

This power may be found on the Board and staff level. On the Board level, are all decisions made by the Executive Committee or by the Board Chair? If so, then this needs to be broadened to include the full Board.

Don't ignore conflicts that may be related to cultural or personal biases with a negative impact on the values of multiculturalism.

At the staff level, who holds power and makes decisions are also important questions to answer as Executive Director. No doubt, as the primary staff leader, you have the ability to lead by example to ensure inclusiveness. If decisions are made by just a few people who also hold the power in your nonprofit, then it will be difficult to have a culture that builds and sustains strong relationships among diverse staff. Your leadership to provide inclusive decision making will create a stronger and healthier organization.

If you find that only a few staff members are really making the decisions in your organization, and that staff are noticeably segregated, then your leadership is crucial to making the decision-making process more inclusive. One idea is to form small groups or teams to work on some projects and make decisions together. Bringing diverse backgrounds into the group will help to achieve your goals of evenly distributed power and integration. Forming teams may also generate some creative thinking and great new ideas!

The work group or team idea works best if staff members have developed a good understanding of the norms of their colleagues. As the Executive Director, you can lead discussions among the staff of diverse work styles, communication preferences, conflict resolution methods, and biases that members of the work group have. It's also useful to hold bigger discussions together with the whole staff as well. Perhaps you could spend time at every staff meeting exploring one of the topics related to diversity, with each person giving their thoughts, while you maintain good ground rules that enable staff to feel comfortable and safe as they speak. The Recommended Resources section for this chapter lists some of the numerous materials available on these topics that provide good exercises for encouraging a better understanding.

Creating a culture that allows for good relationships to be established among all staff will ensure that you are better able to hire and retain a diverse group. Many Executive Directors have asked us for tips on hiring more individuals reflective of their community for their staff. We find that what many of these EDs hope to do is find ways to increase ethnic diversity. It's important to remember that while having an ethnically diverse staff is part of being broadly represented, it's not the only part. Executive Directors should strive to have a staff that is fully representative of the community being served by the nonprofit. Having a strong diversity plan in place is the beginning of increasing diversity. A good diversity plan, though, doesn't mean you are open to broad representation.

The best thing you can do to increase diversity is to make sure you create the most appropriate culture first, before launching a recruitment drive for new paid and unpaid staff and Board members. It is the culture that allows for positive relationships to become established.

Here are some ways to start strengthening your organization's culture to be more accepting of diversity: Invest in training that explores all aspects of diversity and multicultural thinking. Besides formal training, discuss your organization's philosophy and values with staff and others. Stress the importance of including values and beliefs on diversity. Bring staff and volunteers together for exercises or social experiences that surface differences. Structure the time for staff to fully understand and begin to appreciate new ways of thinking, working, and behaving with others. Ways to do this might include having each staff person develop a life map and tell their history to others, or relationship-building exercises to learn about commonalities and differences while also overcoming assumptions they may have had.

Do not allow a culture to develop where staff talk about others who are different in a joking or derogatory way. Personnel policies should reflect an intolerance of this behavior, and the Executive Director should act appropriately to stop it.

How can an Executive Director be a positive role model in encouraging inclusion and diversity?

Good leadership in a broadly represented organization requires the Executive Director to live the desired culture from day to day, in all interactions with Board members, staff, and clients. This is easier said than done.

Understanding your own biases about race, religion, gender, age, disabilities, and other potential areas for discrimination is important. It is the rare person who does not bring some inherent bias from their upbringing. Does your bias come out in anything you say or do in the workplace? If you find you are treating people differently or expecting different work quality from anyone, or making inappropriate remarks, then you will need to change before the culture will change. An Executive Director's insensitivity sets the tone for the whole organization.

Story from the Field

A couple of years ago, Mim facilitated a staff retreat where one topic was improving communication among the twenty-five staff members. This was an ethnically diverse organization, but it was far from being accepting of broad representation; its informal relationships created some enormous communication barriers. One group of employees, including management and line staff, was barely civil to another group. The Executive Director attributed the split to "ethnic differences."

In the retreat, we explored communication styles and some of the barriers that staff members were feeling. As people became more comfortable with the topic and realized the Executive Director was actually listening to their concerns, it came out that a major barrier was how the ED was treating some of the staff. Because of a bias he held (which he acknowledged), this Executive Director communicated less with and expected less from one ethnic group in the organization. His bias was subtle, but staff picked up on it and the result was an organizational culture that split one group from another, and reduced everyone's ability to work together well. While it was very difficult for this talented Executive Director to recognize and accept his bias, the fact that he did so meant that his organizational culture could change through new attitudes and practices to a more positive one.

Another way Executive Directors can be positive role models in encouraging inclusion is to encourage the mentoring of individuals from diverse backgrounds in the organization. When you establish a mentoring process and ensure full inclusion, then you are making it very clear that your leadership is blind to color, age, gender, religion, disability, and the like.

Another way to be a positive role model is to encourage staff and Board members to join and participate in the activities of other nonprofits or membership groups that promote the values of multiculturalism. These groups offer learning opportunities as well as opportunities to share information about your own organization. These learnings can be brought back and discussed with staff, volunteers, and Board members to help them expand their knowledge as well.

How does an Executive Director manage diversity-related conflicts in an organization?

An Executive Director needs to ensure that paid and unpaid staff and Board members can express divergent opinions in a safe manner, and be respected for speaking up. This can, however, lead to conflict. If the conflict is not handled immediately, then it will escalate into a potentially ugly and divisive situation that will be hard to manage.

As with all conflict resolution, there is a first step of discovery where it is important to identify the root of the conflict. It may arise because of a derogatory comment, or a perceived act of favoritism, or any number of other possibilities. The Executive Director needs to demonstrate sensitivity in understanding the perceptions, feelings, and commentary that surround the conflict. These may be filters screening a deeper issue that has to do with the informal relationships, communication styles, decision-making processes, or even images of success that are part of an organization's culture.

Wisdom

Spend time reflecting on your own biases that might reduce your ability to lead your organization toward a culture that values broad representation.

It is important for the Executive Director to keep this big-picture perspective while also learning what the individuals in conflict perceive to be happening. By pointing out the bigger picture and at the same time not diminishing the importance of each person's perspective, an Executive Director is often able to move staff members and Board from conflict to a more positive level of interaction. Common ground can be sought through a discussion with these individuals about what may be done to change the organizational culture to reduce the possibility of future incidents.

Of course, you may also have a staff member, or more than one, who simply does not hold the values of the organization. Conflict may then arise over differing values or personal biases that surface. In these cases, the Executive Director should reinforce the values of the organization and make it clear that all staff must follow and live those values while at work.

So the two different types of conflict regarding broad representation that may arise are conflict stemming from an organizational culture that does not support or honor differences, and conflict stemming from individuals who do not hold the values of a multicultural organization. Both require strong leadership to resolve the differences reflected. How do you tell which kind of conflict is happening? Is the conflict due to organizational culture or personal bias? One way to sort out the type of conflict is by reflecting on these questions:

- According to their own comments on surveys or through direct feedback, do *all* staff feel valued?
- Is staff turnover in the organization relatively low compared to other nonprofits in the area? Are the people who are leaving from a variety of backgrounds?
- Are all appropriate staff providing input into decisions that affect them?
- Do the people being promoted reflect the diversity in the organization?
- Is there zero tolerance in the organization for inappropriate comments and jokes?
- Are staff members communicating with one another regularly in a positive and constructive manner?
- Do the organizational values reflect those of the communities you serve? Does everyone know these values?
- Is there a common understanding that broad representation brings numerous benefits to the organization in addition to the diversity?

If the answer is yes to these questions, then it is likely the conflict is related to differing values and personal biases rather than an organization-wide cultural issue.

Openly discussing and recognizing diversity issues makes the Executive Director's life easier, and makes the organizational environment more pleasant for everyone. Making sure Board and staff have a clear understanding that conflicts may be culture-related rather than person-related will lessen the possibility of repeat issues being raised.

If you find yourself with the task of adapting the organization's culture to make it accepting of diversity and thereby improve relationships, then read Chapter Nine on leading organizational change to help you plot the best strategy to move forward.

PART SIX

Executive Director as Resource Wizard

The highest use of capital is not to make more money, but to make money do more for the betterment of life.

—HENRY FORD

NONPROFIT ORGANIZATIONS are incredible vehicles that allow communities to show their care and concern for others by giving of their time, talent, and resources. Nonprofit leaders, in turn, transform individual and community philanthropy into responsive programs and services that by law are held to a high level of accountability.

We purposely chose the term *wizard* in the title to reflect the amazing ability of Executive Directors who mix and match dozens of funding streams, each with different expectations, time frames, and reporting requirements and transform them into innovative programs that make a difference in the lives of those they serve.

Chapter Sixteen addresses the most common concerns EDs raise in managing the business side of the nonprofit. In Chapter Seventeen, we demystify the process of fundraising and help the ED develop a team-based approach within an organization.

Ensuring Sound Financial Management

by Elizabeth N. Schaffer

Your organization is a mission-based business, not a charity.

—PETER BRINCKERHOFF,
Mission-Based Management

AS AN EXECUTIVE DIRECTOR, you are constantly balancing the pursuit of the mission and the financial sustainability of your organization. Financial oversight cannot be delegated; it lies at the heart of your accountability to your Board, your stakeholders, and your nonprofit's legal requirement to uphold the public trust.

Your specific financial tasks will vary based on your organization's history, culture, and resources, so it isn't possible to cover all the details. However, this chapter addresses some key financial management activities and questions that Executive Directors typically ask as they work their way through financial details:

Wisdom

Develop or clarify mutually agreed-upon annual goals as a basis for your budgeting plan *before* you start to focus on the numbers.

- What are the major differences between for-profit and nonprofit finances?
- Who takes the lead in fulfilling the various financial management roles in a nonprofit?
- What is the Board's role in the budgeting process?
- After the Board passes a budget, what authority does the Executive Director have to implement programs or contracts?
- What should an Executive Director do if it looks like someone has misappropriated funds or resources?
- What financial reports do the Board, staff, and volunteers need to see and how often?
- If there is a financial crisis, what does the Executive Director tell the Board and staff?
- How do nonprofits determine their fiscal year?

Before trying to answer these questions, it is helpful to define the key activities of nonprofit financial management: budgeting, implementation, reporting, and analysis.

Budgeting: The budget is simply your plan for the coming year expressed in terms of income and expenses. In many organizations, the budget cycle represents the bulk of the annual planning effort. Budgeting activities include creating an annual program plan, estimating expenses, and forecasting revenue.

Implementation: Once a budget is in place, you'll begin implementing programs, raising and spending money as approved, and recording financial transactions.

Reporting: At the end of each month and quarter, your accounting staff or service will create reports that reflect all of the month's financial activity.

Analysis: Using the reports, you, the treasurer, and other Board and staff members will monitor financial performance and assess whether the original plan (and budget) is still the best course.

What are the major differences between for-profit and nonprofit finances?

Good financial systems and accounting practices in nonprofit organizations are, for the most part, very similar to those used in the for-profit world. Nonetheless, those new to the nonprofit sector—both officers and Board members—often struggle with how nonprofit financial information is presented. The key differences are the classification of net assets, accounting for contributions, and recording of functional expenses.

Classification of Net Assets: The difference between a nonprofit's assets (property) and liabilities (debt) is known as its net assets. Nonprofit accounting conventions require that (audited) financial statements segregate net assets into three categories:

Ensure that you, staff leadership, and Board members are educated consumers of financial data.

- Unrestricted net assets: Net assets that are not subject to donor-imposed restrictions and can be used at the discretion of Board and management.

- Temporarily restricted net assets: Net assets that are subject to donor-imposed stipulations that may be met by actions of the organization or will be met by the passage of time. When the restriction expires, temporarily restricted net assets are reclassified as unrestricted. For example, say a foundation gives you a two-year grant (time restriction) targeted to the youth development program (purpose restriction). As you implement the program and spend money hiring staff, creating marketing materials, you will release these funds from restriction.

- Permanently restricted net assets: Net assets subject to donor-imposed stipulations that they be maintained permanently by the organization (endowments). The organization can spend the income these assets generate, but cannot dip into the principal sums.

Accounting for Contributions: Nonprofits fund their activities with either earned revenue (client fees, ticket sales, government contracts, and so on) or support (grants and contributions). Accounting for contributions is unique to the nonprofit sector and often misunderstood.

The level of restriction associated with a grant or contribution determines *how* it is recorded. According to generally accepted accounting principles for nonprofit organizations, support is reported in the following three categories:

- *Unrestricted support:* Grants and contributions given by the donor without reference to a specific purpose or use within a specific time period are recorded when pledged and increase the unrestricted net assets of the organization.

- *Temporarily restricted support:* Grants and contributions that are to be spent for a specific purpose or during a restricted period of time are also recorded when pledged and increase the temporarily restricted net assets. Once any restrictions have been met, the grant or contribution will be released (or transferred) into unrestricted net assets, with a corresponding reduction in temporarily restricted net assets.

- *Permanently restricted support:* These are grants and contributions whose principal is to be invested according to the donor's wishes and are added to the permanently restricted new assets when pledged.

Functional Expenses: As defined by the IRS Form 990 and FASB 117, nonprofits must report their expenses by functional classification: program services and supporting services. Exhibit 16.1 provides a detailed breakout of functional expenses. In general, however, *program services* are "the activities that result in goods and services being distributed to beneficiaries, customers, or members that fulfill the purposes or mission for which the organization exists. Those services are the major output of the organization and often relate to several major programs."

Exhibit 16.1 Functional Expense Classifications

Program	Costs resulting in distributing goods and services to clients and fulfilling the mission of the organization.
Administration *(supporting)*	Those costs not identifiable with programs, fundraising, or membership development *and* indispensable to the organization's existence such as governance (that is, Board-related expenses), finance and accounting, legal, and executive management.
Fundraising *(supporting)*	Cost associated with soliciting contributions from individuals, foundations, and corporations; maintaining donor mailing lists; and conducting fundraising events.
Membership Development *(supporting)*	Those costs related to soliciting for prospective members and membership dues, membership relations, and similar activities.

Supporting services are "all activities of a not-for-profit organization other than program services. Generally, they include administration, fundraising, and membership development activities."

Who takes the lead in fulfilling the various financial management roles in a nonprofit?

Nonprofit financial management is a team process that involves both the Board and staff in planning and implementation, as well as in the reporting and monitoring systems that ensure financial stability and public accountability. While these roles will vary to some degree based on your organization's size, culture, and lines of authority, the chart in Exhibit 16.2 will help guide your organization in determining leadership roles and shared responsibilities. On the staff side, the ED may delegate the responsibility to the appropriate financial or program staff within the organization. On the governance side, the Board often delegates the role to the Treasurer or the Finance Committee. While the ED

Exhibit 16.2 Fiscal Roles and Responsibilities

Overall

Goal: To ensure that the organization has fiscal processes and systems that support appropriate control and oversight.

Process: The Board and staff will create a partnership with clearly defined roles and responsibilities.

	Executive Director *(or Delegate)*	Board *(or Delegate)*
Form a Finance Committee.		Lead
Establish meaningful dialog between finance, program, and development staff and committees.	Shared	Shared
Establish salary ranges for each job category; ensure that salaries are within approved ranges.	Shared	Shared
Prepare an annual schedule showing each staff person's category and salary range (for Personnel or Finance Committee, or both).	Lead	

Budgeting and Planning

Goal: To ensure that the organization's budget reflects its mission, values, and overall plan.

Process: The Board and staff will create an inclusive and program-centered budgeting process.

	Executive Director *(or Delegate)*	Board *(or Delegate)*
Create long-range plan, annual goals, and budgeting parameters.		Lead
Develop annual program plan and estimate costs.	Lead	
Create revenue and fundraising projections.	Shared	Shared
Propose plan and budget for approval.	Lead	
Approve the plan and budget; give staff authority to make minor changes.		Lead

Exhibit 16.2 Fiscal Roles and Responsibilities (continued)

Record Keeping

Goal: To appropriately record all financial transactions and safeguard the assets of the organization.

Process: The organization will establish adequate internal controls and ensure that the financial records are accurate and complete.

	Executive Director (or Delegate)	Board (or Delegate)
Develop a written set of internal policies for handling deposits and payments; follow procedures in spirit as well as to the letter.	Lead	
Review and approve key accounting policies.		Lead
Authorize bills and invoices for payment; determine expense coding.	Lead	
Determine appropriate revenue coding for deposits.	Lead	

Reporting

Goals: To summarize the organization's financial position in an accurate and complete manner.

          To comply with all legal and funding requirements.

Process: The staff will regularly produce financial reports that are easily understood and meaningful.

          If needed, the Board will contract with an external accountant to complete or compile an annual audit.

	Executive Director (or Delegate)	Board (or Delegate)
Create monthly financial reports within three weeks of month-end.	Lead	
Distribute financial statements before Board and committee meetings.	Lead	

Exhibit 16.2 Fiscal Roles and Responsibilities (continued)

	Executive Director (or Delegate)	Board (or Delegate)
Prepare brief, written narrative analysis to accompany financial reports.	Lead	
Determine whether an audit is required; select the auditor; receive the audit letter directly from the auditor; meet with the auditor with no staff present (at least once per year).		Lead
Ensure that the audit is completed within four months of fiscal year-end; prepare a written response to comments in the management letter.	Lead	
Complete all legal and funding requirements (or verify that they are completed) in an accurate and timely fashion.	Shared	Shared

Monitoring

Goal: To ensure adequate fiscal oversight.

Process: The staff and Board will review, analyze, and discuss the financial records and reports.

	Executive Director (or Delegate)	Board (or Delegate)
Carefully review organization's financial information.	Shared	Shared
Compare actual results to budget; propose revised plan or budget, or both.	Lead	
Propose items for ad hoc investigation.	Shared	Shared

and Board may delegate certain tasks and responsibilities, they are still ultimately responsible for the oversight and overall accountability of the organization.

What is the Board's role in the budgeting process?

The best budgeting process is a partnership between Board and staff. The first and most important step of the budgeting process is for Board and ED to jointly develop a set of overall assumptions about funding and expenses and to clarify fiscal goals for the upcoming year. If you have a strategic plan in place, it may be simple to agree on these goals. Without a strategic plan, developing the annual goals can be a time-consuming and highly iterative process.

> **Wisdom**
>
> Clarify in writing the Executive Director's authority and any limitations regarding long-term contracts, approval of payments, and unbudgeted expenses.

Once the Board and Executive Director agree on the overall budgeting direction, the next step is to create program and implementation plans. Next, staff leadership in conjunction with Board committees—Executive, Finance, Program, and Development—develop an initial budget draft with a list of budget assumptions. Then, the Board or a designated committee discusses and edits the list, and finally the full Board meets to approve the budget. In approving the budget, the Board is taking the following steps:

- Agreeing to the plan
- Authorizing implementation of that plan
- Expecting that staff will report and analyze financial data to ensure alignment with the plan

Unfortunately, most organizations do not begin the budgeting process by developing or clarifying mutually agreed-upon annual goals.

More typically they just look at the numbers. As a result, the Board meeting to review the budget often turns into a heated discussion as participants challenge details and dollars without the structure and support of an underlying plan. This scenario is best avoided by involving the Board and staff members at the beginning of the budgeting process.

As Executive Director, your particular budget tasks will vary based on the size of your organization. If your organization is small, you may be crunching the numbers and linking the spreadsheets yourself. Regardless of organization size, you should be expected to create the underlying operating plan and to validate all assumptions that are made in response to economic and financial trends.

After the Board passes a budget, what authority does the Executive Director have to implement programs or contracts?

With an approved budget, the Executive Director normally has the authority to execute the plan. You can spend and raise the money represented in the plan—as long as your actions are consistent with the explicit and implicit budget assumptions. For example, this year's budget may include a slot for a new program assistant that is to be funded by a new foundation grant. Although it's not an explicit budget assumption, the Board may expect that you won't fill this position until you receive the grant.

WARNING

Never approve a budget that undermines the long-term financial health of the organization.

It is common and beneficial to have written policies that clarify the Executive Director's authority and any limitations regarding long-term contracts, approval of payments, and unbudgeted expenses.

As you begin to implement your budget, you'll need to continually verify that your original plan is still valid and that the assumptions still work. If you find that your plan or assumptions need updating, be sure to communicate swiftly and clearly about the changes. You'll probably need to engage jointly—with the

Board and key staff—in a planning process to update your goals, your program and development plan, the assumptions, and the budget.

What should an Executive Director do if it looks like someone has misappropriated funds or resources?

Unfortunately, fraud happens all too frequently in non-profit organizations. The best practice is of course to avoid situations that put the organization's assets at risk. Even in small organizations, it is essential to segregate duties and ensure that appropriate checks and balances limit any one individual's access or authority. Often your auditor will conduct an assessment of your systems and provide you with a set of best practices.

WARNING

Never view financial management as someone else's job.

If you ever suspect fraud, you'll want to immediately take the following steps:

1. Notify your Board Chair, Treasurer, auditor, and the full Executive Committee.
2. Contact an attorney.
3. Involve the police in your investigation.
4. Evaluate and change the procedures involved.
5. If guilt is determined, fire the person immediately.

Story from the Field

A few years ago, Liz was on the Board of an organization with a passionate and committed Office Manager who supervised the receptionist, ordered supplies, and handled most of the day-to-day financial transactions. With the Board's approval, he had obtained a company credit card to facilitate supply orders.

One day when the Office Manager was out sick, the Clinic Director noticed a stack of unopened mail sitting on the Office Manager's desk. She asked the Receptionist about it and was told that the Office Manager always opened the mail. Her curiosity piqued, she opened the credit card bill and found that more than $5,000 worth of computers had been charged!

After a few deep breaths, she called the credit card company to explain that there was an error, and she was told that equipment had been purchased over the last six months. She requested that the statements be faxed to her, and she quickly saw that a pattern had been building over the last few months. She also found the payments—small checks every week that she had signed! Needless to say, the Office Manager was asked not to return to work and was turned into the local police. Unfortunately, the agency never recovered any of the funds!

In this case, the Office Manager did not sign checks, but he opened the mail, wrote the checks, and received the bank statements—too much control for any one set of hands, no matter how trustworthy they seem.

All Executive Directors, but especially those in small organizations, need to be involved in and attentive to what is occurring around them. If you're not familiar with any of the transactions on which you are asked to sign off, ask. Better to be safe than sorry.

WARNING

Never withhold critical financial information from Board and staff.

What financial reports do the Board, staff, and volunteers need to see and how often?

The only report that nonprofit organizations are required to file (and then, only those with receipts of more than $25,000) is IRS Form 990. Unfortunately, although satisfying legal requirements is essential, most organizations cannot use the Form 990 as a management tool. Regardless of the organization's income level, Board and staff need other financial information to let them know how things are going. Typically, the Board and staff will want answers to these questions:

- Do we have enough money?
- Are our results consistent with our plan or budget?
- Do we need a new plan?
- What's our cash flow situation?

You'll need to be able to answer these questions as frequently as things change in your organization. When you can't locate an answer in your head, it is time to find the answer elsewhere. For most organizations, a small group—such as the staff leadership team or the Board's Finance Committee—reviews data on a monthly basis. For other organizations a more comprehensive quarterly presentation to the full Board with an update for all staff works well. Typically, the organization's external constituencies—funders, members, donors, and so on—expect an annual financial update. Most important is to create a schedule and stick to it. When folks expect data and don't receive it, they tend to think the worst.

The chart in Exhibit 16.3 provides an example of who needs to know what financial information in the typical nonprofit organization.

The Executive Director's key role in financial reporting is to ensure that everyone—ED, staff leadership, and Board members alike—upholds the public trust. All parties must be educated consumers of financial data and accountable to the organization's stakeholders.

If there is a financial crisis, what does the Executive Director tell the Board and staff?

When the news spreads that an organization is in financial crisis, what does it mean? It might mean that a significant source of funding was cut, and now there are not enough resources available to maintain programs.

Exhibit 16.3 Financial Information Communication Chart

Audience	Type of Data	Frequency
Management Team	• Statement of activities (income statement) by department with budget comparisons	Monthly
Finance Committee	• Statement of activities with budget comparison	Monthly
	• Statement of functional expenses	
	• Statement of financial position (balance sheet)	
	• Cash flow projection	
Full Board	• Statement of activities with budget comparison	Quarterly
	• Statement of financial position	
	• Cash flow projection	
Funders, members, donors	• Audited statement of activities	Annually
	• Audited statement of financial position	

It might mean that the organization is unable to meet its financial obligations. It might mean that someone has defrauded the organization. More often than not, it is one of these scenarios coupled with a lack of information about the financial situation. The best advice in a crisis: whether the news is bad or good, use the same reporting process. Stick to the schedule and keep the information flowing.

Unfortunately, in a crisis, there is typically no data at all. In this case, the sooner you get data, the better. As the Executive Director, you will want to model the best practice of making decisions based on data, not assumptions. And no matter how bad the news, the best practice is to be honest with both Board and staff.

THE EXECUTIVE DIRECTOR'S SURVIVAL GUIDE

How do nonprofits determine their fiscal year?

The fiscal year is an accounting convention for accumulating and reporting data. An organization should choose its fiscal year based on program needs and funding streams. Schools often base their choice on the academic calendar, August 1 to July 31; organizations that receive the bulk of their revenue from the federal government may choose to align with the government cycle, October 1 to September 30. Many municipalities and foundations use a fiscal year that runs from July 1 to June 30, and many nonprofits have followed suit without considering their own unique needs.

If your program runs year-round and you have no other compelling reason to choose an alternative, the calendar year is often easiest, as you have to keep your payroll records on this cycle anyway. By filing a few IRS forms, you can change your fiscal year to reflect the cycle that makes the best sense for your organization.

Changing your fiscal year makes year-to-year comparisons initially more complicated; however, the other advantages may make changing be quite worthwhile. For example, if your organization has a major annual fundraising event at the beginning or end of the fiscal year, record keeping can be cumbersome—event revenue would be split over fiscal periods and statements may not match development records. As Executive Director, you'll want to ensure that the fiscal year is appropriate for your organization—and that both planning and implementing cycles feel right.

Wisdom

The ED's job is to ensure that the organization balances its heart or mission with a sound fiscal plan.

CHAPTER SEVENTEEN

Sustaining the Organization with Team-Based Fundraising

Of all the factors that contribute to sustained success in fund raising, none may be more important than creating a cohesive and effective development team.

—KAY SPRINKEL GRACE, in *Achieving Excellence in Fundraising*

RAISING FUNDS is both a joy and a curse for Executive Directors. The joy comes when you are successful in sharing your passion and vision for the organization with the community, who in turn invest in your mission with a grant, major gift, or some other challenging donation. The curse comes when you feel that your entire job is about fundraising, and things aren't going well.

The reality is that Executive Directors need to know a lot about fundraising, but they don't have sole responsibility for making sure the organization always has enough funds.

This chapter provides insights that will help Executive Directors create a team to raise funds. Our belief is that this all-important task is one that everyone in the nonprofit can be involved in. These are the questions answered here:

- Who has the primary responsibility for raising money in a nonprofit?
- How much of an Executive Director's time should be spent raising money?
- Where do nonprofits find funds for overhead costs of administration and building infrastructure?

Much of the material in this chapter comes from the book *Team Based Fundraising: Step by Step,* written by one of the coauthors of this book, Mim Carlson.

Who has the primary responsibility for raising money in a nonprofit?

The Executive Director isn't the only person with significant responsibility for fundraising. The Board of Directors shares this responsibility, because it is the Board that ultimately must keep the doors open and programs operating. If board members are not supporting fundraising in some way, they are not doing their job.

Wisdom

It is important for your organization to operate in a fundraising culture that has Board, staff, and volunteers involved in finding funds. Fundraising is not just the Executive Director's job.

We view fundraising as a team effort between Board members, the Executive Director, and to a lesser extent, others in an organization. Whether you are identifying prospective donors, cultivating them, asking for contributions, or recognizing donor generosity, each person on the team shares the responsibility for making sure that fundraising activities are carried out and that goals are being achieved.

For a team approach to fundraising to work well in any nonprofit, a good understanding of roles among all the members of the team is essential. It is best to develop a brief matrix like the one shown in Exhibit 17.1 to summarize key team member roles in fundraising.

Exhibit 17.1 Fundraising Team Responsibilities Matrix

Who	What
Team Leader: Board Chair	• Sets the example for the full Board in terms of performance. • Builds commitment among Board members and makes sure that the skills and experience of Board members are matched to the tasks they perform. • Remains conscious that fundraising is only one of the essential duties of the Board of Directors.
Team Leader: Executive Director	• Sets the example for the rest of the staff in terms of performance. • Demonstrates enthusiasm about the goals, builds commitment among staff to raise funds, and effectively matches skills and experience to the tasks that need to be carried out. • Focuses on the staff's performance. • Manages the process of team selection and ensures effectiveness of the team.
Directors	• Accept training to increase skills and become more effective. • *Identify:* Provide names of colleagues, businesses, and others who might be prospects for development. • *Cultivate:* Serve on task forces matching interests and skills. • *Ask:* Obtain donations and make donations themselves. • *Recognize:* Thank donors for their generosity. • *Monitor:* Set fundraising policies with staff.
Staff	• Accept training to increase skills and become more effective. • *Identify:* See every contact as a potential donor; track donor data. • *Cultivate:* Provide information about constituent needs and service quality and about program results that are making a difference in the community; demonstrate those positive results and thus provide a reason for donors to give; communicate to potential and current donors that their nonprofit operates smoothly and is professionally managed. • *Ask:* Visit with donors and prospects to provide details of the organization's work. • *Recognize:* Thank donors they know for their generosity.
Non-Board volunteers	• Accept training to increase skills and become more effective. • *Identify:* Introduce their places of employment to the nonprofit's mission to generate contributions, develop list of contacts for solicitations and maintain the donor database and research prospective donors. • *Cultivate:* Serve on task forces according to interest and skills. • *Ask:* Solicit friends, family, work colleagues, and neighbors to become donors; organize special events; make financial contributions of their own. • *Recognize:* Thank donors they know for their gifts.

Members of the leadership group have some very specific responsibilities to be aware of. In this context, we're referring to the Board Chair, the chair of the Board's Fundraising Committee, the Executive Director, and the Development Director (if an organization has a paid or unpaid staff person in this role). This group provides management through planning, monitoring, and implementing. It provides leadership through motivating, supporting, and encouraging the team.

Team members can determine their responsibilities in these four key fundraising areas: identifying donors, cultivating them, asking for contributions, and recognizing donor generosity.

As the chart in the exhibit indicates, everyone has a role in fundraising. It is your leadership, as Executive Director, that creates the culture of a fundraising team and ensures that everyone supports one another as well as meeting their own responsibilities as team members. Strong communication skills and the desire to work through others to raise funds are very important for the busy Executive Director, who cannot possibly do all the fundraising in the nonprofit.

WARNING

Be wary of an Executive Director job description or work plan that designates a percentage of your time for fundraising. Your time for this task varies depending on the financial status of your organization.

How much of an Executive Director's time should be spent raising money?

Although we are asked this question often, it is difficult to answer because circumstances are different in every nonprofit. In all nonprofits, you spend time as a leader providing vision, motivation, and strategic thinking to the task of fundraising. You also raise money and are a leader on the fundraising team. Some organizations, though, have a lesser need for fundraising because of where they are in their life cycle, so it is a lower priority. Others base their existence on raising funds so it is a higher priority.

For instance, as an Executive Director of a land trust, with no other staff, you are going to spend a majority of your time on some aspect of raising funds because that is what fulfills the purpose of the trust (to purchase land or easements for protecting open space). On the other hand, as an ED of a large social services agency with many programs and numerous staff you may spend less time raising money because government contracts pay for most of the services, and you have numerous other demands on your time as you work to fulfill the mission of the organization. Also, a nonprofit early in its life cycle or when going through a heavy growth period will need an Executive Director who spends more time finding and building relationships with donors, while an ED leading a nonprofit later in its life cycle may find that those relationships have stabilized and thus demand less time.

But remember that wherever the organization is in its life cycle, the Board, staff, community volunteers, and other key stakeholders are participating too. The Executive Director is a leader and a manager, but not the solo solicitor.

As you work to figure out how much time you should be spending on fundraising, ask yourself the following questions and consider some ideas to manage your time on this task.

- *Are there times during the year when you have noticed that more fundraising tasks need to be done?* If so, plan ahead and have a team working on some of those tasks so it is not just your job to write those grant proposals, facilitate the direct mail appeal, or get major gifts.
- *Is someone on staff—or perhaps a volunteer—eager to build fundraising skills?* Does that person seem to have the capacity to do so? If yes, then mentor them with training and chances to work alongside you.
- *Do you find that fundraising is consuming so much of your time that other priorities are not being met?* If yes, then it is time for a

heart-to-heart with your Board. If the relationship is a healthy partnership, then your Board is there to support and encourage you—and to do their fair share of fundraising.

- *Does everyone know what is involved with the task of fundraising at your organization, and how much time it consumes?* If not, then it is time to communicate and educate staff, Board, and volunteers about the many facets of raising money. It is also a good idea to talk about fundraising and create a plan to involve more of your organization in the task.

Remember always that your primary job at your organization is to be a leader. This goes for fundraising as well as all other tasks you do.

Where do nonprofits find funds for overhead costs of administration and building infrastructure?

This question often comes up when Executive Directors are stretched to the limit with providing programs and want some more administrative dollars to build structures to support those programs. The term *unrestricted* is often used to define these funds because it is money that can be used for any purpose in the nonprofit.

The real time to be thinking about finding unrestricted money is before you really need it. The reason for this is that the search for unrestricted funds can be a long one and generally takes the time of everyone in your organization.

Unrestricted funds come primarily from individual donors to your nonprofit. To a much lesser extent, they come from ongoing foundation support, service clubs, small businesses, and groups that have philanthropic dollars to give away. Much has been written on how to raise money from individuals and groups, and you will find our favorite guides in this chapter's section of the Recommended Resources at the end of the book.

Instead, the focus here is on ways that you can create a culture in your nonprofit that supports obtaining individual or other donor gifts. This is important because nonprofits that find themselves in need of unrestricted funds have usually relied heavily on grant funds or government contracts that direct the majority of their dollars directly to programs and require different relationships and skills. New systems and skills to target individual donors, track donations, and recognize gifts need to be established.

Story from the Field

An experienced Executive Director took a new ED position in a stable, mature organization that had always relied on government contracts with minimal foundation grant support. One of her new priorities was to bring in unrestricted funds to increase the administrative support. The new ED unwisely agreed to a substantial goal of $100,000 in one year in unrestricted gifts. But wisely, she said that the Board and staff needed to participate in achieving the goal. The Board agreed to this.

The Executive Director made the assumption that the Board and staff would be interested in raising funds, and that the organization had a database of potential donors, as well as systems for tracking gifts, communicating about progress, and the like. But the organization had never seen the need to have the necessary database or systems, nor had anyone in it any experience in asking for money, so there was, in fact, nothing in place.

Rather than setting herself up to fail with a $100,000 goal and no way to achieve it, the Executive Director went back to her Board with an analysis of the situation and a proposal. She outlined what it would take financially and in terms of time to move the organization to being able to reach the Board's original goal. The

Wisdom

Finding unrestricted funds to support overhead costs requires special systems that help to identify and track donor contributions and ensure good recognition of their gifts. If your organization has always been grant dependent, time is needed to shift systems to support asking for and receiving individual donations.

Board accepted her proposal and learned about the realities of switching to a culture of raising unrestricted funds.

The lesson here is to set funding goals that match your capacity to achieve them. To raise unrestricted gifts, you need, at a minimum, to have individuals, groups, and businesses to solicit and to have them in an easily accessible and up-to-date database. You also need a plan for soliciting and people to carry out the plan. Are you going to use events, face-to-face requests, fundraising letters, phone calls, or what? You also need a good system to track the gifts when they come in, and a good recognition strategy to ensure that everyone gets thanked no matter what size their gift.

This is a lot to put in place if you are a busy Executive Director with many other matters to attend to, so the team concept of fundraising is what makes the most difference here. It should not be your job to set up a database, track donors, solicit them, recognize them, communicate with them regularly about your organization's accomplishments, and all the other things that need to happen in a solid unrestricted gift program. The chart in Exhibit 17.2, from *Team-Based Fundraising: Step by Step,* identifies ways others in the organization can turn your dream of getting unrestricted gifts into a reality. We recommend that Executive Directors share this survey with Board and staff and begin to build a team on the interests expressed by each person.

To use the chart in the exhibit effectively, ask everyone who is part of the fundraising team to fill it out individually. Then the team leadership can compile the information and create an unrestricted donations plan that allows people to do what best matches their skills and interests.

Fundraising can be fun and rewarding for Executive Directors and for everyone in the organization who participates. Since this is the critical task that keeps the doors open and the programs operating, it needs to be a shared responsibility to be truly successful.

Exhibit 17.2 Team Involvement in Unrestricted Gifts

Team Member Name _____

Team Goal: To obtain unrestricted gifts

Objective	Task	Will Do	Maybe— Ask	I'd like to learn how
Systems Development	• Design or modify a database to track unrestricted gifts. • Develop a plan for obtaining donations. • Create evaluation tools to monitor progress.			
Identify Donors	• Provide lists of names. • Research current donors. • Input data into the database. • Assist with database management.			
Cultivation	• Talk to other groups about our organization. • Work on a newsletter task force. • Develop the agency case statement. • Visit prospects. • Work on a legislative task force. • Recruit new volunteers.			
Solicitations	• Organize a major donor drive. • Recruit volunteer solicitors. • Solicit people and groups. • Conduct a phone-a-thon. • Organize a direct mail campaign. • Work on a direct mail campaign. • Help plan special events. • Lead an events committee. • Work at the event.			
Recognize Donors	• Develop recognition events for donors. • Write and send donor thank-you letters.			

Note: This survey is not all-inclusive. Your team will want to add and subtract skills depending on your needs.

PART SEVEN

Executive Director in Transition

A leadership change puts everyone into transition. Handling the change well is only half the solution. The other half is managing the transition.

—William Bridges

No one has a job for life, not even an Executive Director. If you are a strong ED with a long tenure, it is easy for your organization to lose sight of the fact that you will move on at some point. Remember, as ED you are serving as a temporary caretaker of the mission.

Executive Directors outgrow the organizations they lead and some organizations outgrow the skill sets of their current ED. Some EDs need new or different challenges, others find themselves in an organization whose values or culture are not in line with their own. Career transitions are natural, but they're an often-forgotten or uncomfortable topic for many EDs and Boards.

This part of the book attempts to bring the topic out into the open and provide Executive Directors and the organizations where they work with tools and insight to make the inevitable transition a healthy and productive one. We purposely select the term *transition* because it better defines the process as opposed to the outcome of changes in leadership.

Transition, as described by William Bridges, is the psychological and emotional process you, the organization, and its stakeholders go through to come to terms with change. Some move through this process smoothly and with relative ease. Others, particularly those with a strong culture built on long-term relationships, find it difficult, complex, and emotionally exhausting. They need time to feel their emotions, reflect on what the change means to them personally, and come to terms with the professional impact of the transition.

In Chapter Eighteen we help you evaluate if and when to leave. We offer tools and support to both you and your organization. Rather than viewing leadership transitions as a challenge, we encourage you to look at it as a time of growth and reflection for you and your organization. Chapter Nineteen explores career options that build on your nonprofit leadership experience.

CHAPTER EIGHTEEN

Moving On: Leading Your Own Career Transition

Leadership Transition is a powerful opportunity to improve the balance and strengthen an organization. Use this pivotal moment to successfully manage your transition and lead a thriving organization.
— TOM ADAMS, *Transition Guides*

EXECUTIVE DIRECTORS are widely regarded as champions of change in organizations, yet relatively few welcome or spend much time considering their own process of changing jobs. This chapter considers the opportunities and challenges imposed on you and your organization during an Executive Director transition and offers guidance to both the ED and the Board in managing the process. The chapter addresses the following questions:

- When is it time for an Executive Director to consider a career move?
- Why is the decision to leave so difficult for the Executive Director and the organization?

- How should a nonprofit approach succession planning?
- How can the departing Executive Director make the leadership transition run smoothly?

When is it time for an Executive Director to consider a career move?

Perhaps the first question to answer is really "Why does an Executive Director leave a nonprofit?" Have you ever thought about writing a letter of resignation following an unflattering performance review or after an unusually difficult Board meeting? Perhaps you have dreams of pursuing your vision of that idyllic organization with a unified Board, legions of dedicated volunteers, self-directed staff, generous donors, state-of-the-art technology, and, of course, you at the helm in a large corner office with a view.

As we discussed in Chapter Three, burnout in the nonprofit sector is not difficult to understand. The motivating factors that make the nonprofit sector so attractive in the first place—a passion to fulfill a mission and change a community or save the world—often lead people into jobs that take over their lives. On a more practical level, many nonprofit meetings are scheduled before or after business hours or on weekends to accommodate volunteers, and this often significantly extends the length of staff workdays.

The decision to consider a new job option is also driven by internal reflections on staying inspired that we discussed in Chapter Two. In addition to examining barriers to your inspiration, consider your responses to the following fundamental questions:

- Do you still love the work you are doing?
- Are you still passionate about the mission?

Wisdom

It is never too early to think about your own exit strategy, just as there is never a perfect time to leave. At some point you know that moving on is to everyone's benefit.

- Do you enjoy going to work and interacting with your staff, Board, volunteers, and clients?

- Do you believe you are making a difference?

- Do you receive supportive or appreciative feedback from your Board, staff, and stakeholders?

- Are your leadership and management skills appropriate to the stage of development that your organization is moving through?

- Do your career and personal goals complement each other?

If your answers to these questions are mostly no or hesitant yeses, it is time to seriously reflect on your skills and your career and life goals. Are you simply in the wrong agency or in the wrong field? If your answers are mostly yes and you still wonder about your job commitment, answer these questions:

- Would additional support or coaching help you deal with the opportunities and challenges at hand? Chapter Two may offer some additional insight into ways coaching can help.

- Have you ever taken more than one week of vacation? If so, how recently and how did it affect you?

- Is it time to take a sabbatical? That is, a real break—a month or even a six-month inspirational vacation. As one close friend stated following his sabbatical, "The boulders now look more like pebbles and I have a more absorbent wall to bang my head against."

Story from the Field

When Margaret took her first ED job, she made a commitment to the Board to stay for a minimum of five years. Before she knew it she was in her seventh year, suffering from a mild case of the seven-year itch. She was ready for a change, but she was too busy working to pursue even great opportunities. After another year had passed, she found herself feeling apprehensive of launching another strategic plan for the organization. She loved her job, had a talented staff and committed Board, and felt empowered to make a difference, but her interest and ability to lead the organization toward a new vision was weak. Her leadership torch was running out of fuel. With her second child on the way, the daily two-hour commute was no longer "valued alone time" but a barrier to efforts to balance personal and professional life. She needed to find new balance, a new career, and a new vision for herself. She concluded it was time to move on.

Often the decision is driven by new career opportunities; sometimes it will come from internal reflection about your life goals and how your job as an ED complements them or competes with them. There really is no such thing as a perfect time to leave. You will always see opportunities or challenges you'd like to address before leaving your nonprofit. However, having a succession transition plan in place will not only help to ease your departure anxieties and those of your organization, it can also transform your departure into an opportunity for growth and change instead of a crisis.

Warning

Be prepared to have your departure announcement met with some fear, resistance, and possibly anger. Don't take it personally, rather remember that processing of psychological and emotional issues is a healthy and necessary part of any transition.

Once you decide to leave, remember that you can consult a wealth of books, workshops, career counselors, and Web sites that promote career planning and self-reliance. You'll find a few starting points listed among the Recommended Resources for this chapter. In addition, colleagues, mentors, family, and when appropriate your Board can provide you with invaluable feedback and guidance. Refer to Chapter Nineteen for additional insight on options for your next career.

Why is the decision to leave so difficult for the Executive Director and the organization?

There is more to leaving your position as Executive Director than simply writing a letter of resignation, cleaning out your desk, wrapping up loose ends, and celebrating your accomplishments with colleagues. The transition involves more than the simple departure of one key staff member and the subsequent hiring of another. Your departure thrusts the entire organization into a significant period of cultural change. In addition to dealing with your own reactions, you must also deal with the organization's reaction to the loss of a friend, colleague, and leader.

While the decision to leave an organization is not an easy one for most Executive Directors, the fact that you have made the choice to move on provides you with a sense of control. By contrast, your organization finds itself unexpectedly having to deal with the emotional loss of a colleague and the demanding process of filling the leadership void. The longer you have been with the organization, the harder the transition may be. It takes time for staff, volunteers, and Board members to envision the organization without you. Celebrations that recognize your legacy and give you an opportunity to say thank you and good-bye are a critical part of your term's ending and establish a healthy foundation for the next ED to enter.

Wisdom

Encourage the Board and support their efforts to take on leadership of the transition. Yes, you can probably lead the search process more efficiently than they can, but if they are to take ownership of the outcome, they must define and struggle with the issues.

How should a nonprofit approach succession planning?

It isn't a question of *if* you will ever leave the organization, but *when*. Many corporations in today's business world expect their CEOs to form an "exit strategy" shortly after being hired. Why? The goal is not to encourage turnover but rather to acknowledge the need for ongoing planning about the direction and leadership needs of the organization. Incorporating the topic of succession planning into strategic or annual planning reduces staff and Board anxiety and expedites the move to new leadership when the time comes.

Putting issues on the table early on rather than concurrently with your decision to leave is much easier for everyone and optimizes the chances that your organization will successfully navigate its way through your actual departure to a new safe harbor with the next generation of leadership.

For most nonprofit organizations, the term *succession planning* suggests grooming a select individual to become the next Executive Director—but they don't have an obvious candidate and so they wind up with no succession planning at all. Few nonprofit organizations are large enough to have that depth of expertise on staff. Rather, we suggest a more systematic approach to nonprofit succession planning. What systems, relationships, and values can be put in place early in your tenure to ensure a successful leadership transition for everyone later on? To answer this question necessitates a look at your leadership and management roles as well as many of the issues considered in preceding chapters. You will work with your Board throughout the various succession planning processes, gently prompting action in a variety of ways, but leadership must come from the members of the Board. They have many specific tasks they need to complete to ensure a successful leadership transition.

Dealing with the following key issues will help you to establish a strong footing for your organization as it moves through a succession planning process:

1. Understand the changing nonprofit environment and organizational life cycles and how these changes affect your mission and define the skills any Executive Director for your organization should have.

2. Identify and articulate your organization's unique values and culture.

3. Develop realistic job expectations that allow for professional and personal balance.

4. Clarify internal roles and the nature of relationships between the Executive Director and the Board, staff, volunteers, Founder, and stakeholders.

Wisdom

Be clear and definitive about your intention and schedule for leaving.

5. Build a clear and unified vision of where the organization is going and how to measure your effectiveness.

6. Develop an emergency transition plan that will allow for organizational stability in the event of an unexpected transition and give the Board time to develop a long-term plan that addresses conditions at that time.

The checklist in Exhibit 18.1 is designed to help guide the Board through their leadership roles in the event of a transition. (A similar checklist to help guide the ED through the management issues of a transition can be found in Exhibit 18.2 toward the end of this chapter.)

How can the departing Executive Director make the leadership transition run smoothly?

The ending you orchestrate for your leadership term creates the foundation on which the next Executive Director will begin to build. In the context of Board leadership and in consideration of the elements of change discussed in Chapter Nine, the steps discussed in this section will help guide you to a good ending for yourself while the Board focuses on a new beginning for the organization. There are some similarities in the steps, but the focus here is on you and your ability to let go and move on.

Step One: Take care of yourself. Start spending time with yourself. With honesty and clarity, identify your reasons for leaving. Set a definite time line for your departure and avoid the temptation to delay your departure in response to anxieties expressed by your staff or Board members. Sometimes it is difficult to set a departure date because of uncertainty about your future plans. If this is the case, set a date to leave and decide to develop your future plans after you leave.

If you are a Founder or have been with the organization for many years, your identification with the organizational culture may be so strong as to make it especially difficult for people to envision moving

Exhibit 18.1 Board Leadership Transition Checklist

In the event of an ED transition, the Board should consider the following list to guide their work:

Task	Purpose	✔
Form transition committee.	• Evaluate interim management needs. • Manage leadership transition. • Conduct ED search.	
Create a communication plan.	• Promptly communicate the transition to internal and external stakeholders. • Provide reassurance of a plan and leadership for a smooth transition.	
Plan celebration for departing ED.	• Recognize and celebrate ED's legacy.	
Develop interim leadership plan.	• Maintain ongoing operations. • Ensure open communication channels between Board and paid and volunteer staff. • Support processing of emotional and psychological transition issues.	
Evaluate need for outside expertise to guide the Board through the ED search process.	• Ensure adequate resources are in place to support an effective and timely process.	
Assess organizational strengths, challenges, opportunities, and threats.	• Accurately determine skills and experience needed in new ED.	
Revisit strategic plan for clarification of shifts in organizational focus.	• Represent organization accurately.	
Prioritize the essential skills and experience needed in the new ED.	• Ensure a good fit to encourage longer tenure.	
Determine recruitment and selection strategy, including implementation steps.	• Locate a strong pool of qualified candidates.	
Plan new ED orientation.	• Welcome, educate, and support new ED. • Clarify roles, responsibilities, and authority.	
Establish three-month ED performance expectations.	• Clarify priorities and expectations between Board and ED.	
Set first-year schedule for ED quarterly reviews.	• Provide feedback to support and clarify priorities and expectations.	

forward without you. It is both challenging and essential to find a balance between your strong leadership legacy and an objective evaluation of the organization's strengths, weaknesses, opportunities, and barriers to success. Without burning bridges, you must pass the authority to lead the organization forward on to your successor.

Story from the Field

A colleague decided to leave the organization she had been with for more than fifteen years. Since she had no specific plans other than to travel with her family and take time to explore a new career, she did not set a specific date to leave. Instead, she gave the Board over a year's notice, helped them form an active transition committee, removed herself from long-range projects, and focused on wrapping up a laundry list of short-term projects. Although the transition team launched an ED search immediately, twelve months later they still had not found the right person. Tired and frustrated, she finally booked a trip to Europe and announced that she was leaving in sixty days. Her clarity about a departure date enabled the transition team to focus and hire a new Executive Director before she left.

Step Two: Craft a departure communication plan. Who needs to know what and when? Sit down with your Board Chair or Executive Committee and discuss how to share the news of your departure with the rest of the Board, staff, volunteers, and stakeholders. If your departure is imminent—say, six weeks or less—the sooner people know, the sooner the organization can begin the personal and organizational transitions.

If you are able to give longer notice, six months to a year, it is important to guide your Board through the pros and cons of having a lame duck leader and a prolonged transition period. As departing ED, you are often delegated to deal with day-to-day management issues. It no longer makes sense for you to provide leadership on issues that affect the organization's future direction.

Once plans for announcing your departure are determined and made public, encourage your Board leadership to put those plans into writing—summarizing your tenure, accomplishments, future plans, recognition event, time line, and preliminary plans for continuity of leadership. Having a succession plan already in place will of course make this much easier.

Step Three: Transfer leadership. It is time to transfer the leadership reins to the Board. From the moment you announce your intention to leave, you relinquish long-term leadership of the organization and become a sort of interim ED. It is important to remember that your Board will not start to lead the transition process until you let go of the reins. Now is not the time to commit the organization to the details of a new strategic vision that you will not be around to implement, or to launch a new program that is based on your connections and skills.

WARNING

Don't pick your successor. Too often the person you would pick is too similar to you. The selection is the Board's responsibility, and often they need a fresh perspective whether or not they realize they want one.

You continue the day-to-day management of the organization, focusing on the transfer of knowledge, responsibilities, and relationships. You will need to negotiate clear boundaries with the Board for your transitional role, transfer responsibilities for long-range projects to others, and clarify your level of authority on major issues that will affect the organization beyond your tenure.

If you and the Board anticipate a gap of three months or more between your departure and the arrival of the next Executive Director, the Board may want to consider hiring someone else to act as an interim ED. While this may be a new concept for some communities, more and more nationally affiliated and local management support organizations are recruiting and developing seasoned nonprofit professionals to serve in interim management roles so that organizations and Boards have the necessary time to do a comprehensive search and accomplish a smooth leadership transition.

This interval can be especially valuable when Board and staff are dealing with the more intense emotional and organizational issues associated with ending a lengthy relationship with their Executive Director. The downside of having an interim ED is that your organization faces two leadership transitions in a short period of time.

Step Four: Celebrate your legacy. Finally, you get to step back and celebrate your legacy—embrace the relationships you have formed and candidly acknowledge the opportunities and challenges you are passing on to your successor. Then let go. Assuming everyone has paid attention to the details of this transition, the new Executive Director will be able to move into the job with a couple of days of orientation and a few phone calls or meetings a month or so down the road.

Lengthy overlap with the new ED is usually not necessary and can create awkward dual leadership issues for Board and staff. Also avoid the invitation to join the Board or consult, at least initially. While the intent is good, the offer is often a sign of reluctance to accept change. Your tenure is complete and it is now time for your successor to establish a new pattern of identity, authority, and visibility in the organization and the community. The organization should be ready to explore its vision, opportunities, and challenges through new eyes. The next ED will probably approach the organization much differently than you did and that can be very healthy.

Exhibit 18.2 provides a checklist for Executive Directors to orchestrate good endings and help track the many management tasks that need to be done during the transition time. Above all, be clear about your decision to leave. Once you have made that decision, leave with integrity in a time-sensitive manner. Your ultimate legacy and years of hard work will be framed in your ability to make a clean transition.

The actions proposed in Exhibit 18.2 and the information compiled as a result of using it become part of your parting legacy to the organization and form a welcoming foundation for the interim or incoming ED. The new Executive Director's initial success will help put the organization on track for years to come, so the effort is well worthwhile.

How you leave the leadership of an organization is as important as how you enter it. Do it well and it contributes to your legacy and the well-being of those that follow. Do it poorly and your years of accomplishments can be quickly forgotten. Career transitions are never easy to anticipate, but like wills and memorial services are part of the natural progression of life.

> ## Wisdom
> How you leave the leadership of an organization is as important as how you enter it.

Exhibit 18.2 Executive Director Transition Management Checklist

Task	✔
Compile list of pending projects and assignments. Meet with Executive or Transition Committee to set priorities and determine delegation procedures. Set up a transition file to include the following items: • Board roster, job descriptions, and biographies. • Volunteer committee structure and membership. • Staff roster and job descriptions. • Organization chart. • Board and volunteer committee rosters. • Strategic plan or annual goals and accomplishments to date. • Employee handbook. • Most recent budget, financial statements, cash flow statements, and audit. • Bylaws and policies, procedures, or practices not documented elsewhere. • List of vendors, task forces, or collaboratives for which you have primary responsibility. Include contact info and meeting schedules. • Staff, Board, volunteer, and community challenges or threats (prepared in conjunction with Executive Committee). • Brief summary of your typical week and month in terms of Board, staff, clients, reports and administration, and community connections. • Brief summary of key seasonal issues that affect your role. • List of deadlines for reports to funders, stakeholders, community leaders. • Critical info pertaining to voice mail, e-mail, pager, cell phone, alarm system, and bank account numbers and passwords. Complete outstanding employee evaluations and document deficiencies or warnings. Develop a schedule of pending reviews and how they are to be handled. Make the following contacts: • Inform the auditor of the transition and see if you need to gather anything for next year's audit that only you may know. • Change signature authority with all banks and payroll services. • Inform external stakeholders of the transition and assure them that the organization will be in good hands. Transfer your relationship to others in conjunction with the Board communication plan.	

CHAPTER NINETEEN

Envisioning Your Next Career

A job is not an avenue for making money, it's an opportunity to combine your professional and spiritual selves in a meaningful way.
—MARK ALBION, *Finding Work That Matters*

WHILE THE PRIMARY INTENT of this book has been to expand your degree of satisfaction in your current Executive Director position, the reality is that eventually you will be looking for a new job. Our hope is that you will continue in the nonprofit sector and take your leadership skills to another organization, but we know that more than half of Executive Directors have little interest in staying in the role. Delighted as we would be if this book and other support and development resources for EDs could improve on these statistics, we recognize that your ED experience can translate into other fulfilling career options. The focus of this chapter is to help assure you that there is life after your career as an Executive Director.

No one has produced a sure-fire recipe for making a career shift, but many have found that a positive move is always possible. Although many ingredients are needed, you can move onto a path that can bring you even greater rewards and more career satisfaction

Wisdom

If you are serious about making a successful career transition, make it a priority in your calendar every day or week. It is a time-consuming process.

than you have known thus far. According to most books, Web sites, and newsletters on career change, success begins with a desire for change, is sustained by strong commitment and vision, and results in a lifetime of rewarding work.

This chapter assumes that you have recognized a desire for change. To help you focus on "What next?" it raises the following questions:

- What are the first steps to making a career change?
- What kind of support does an Executive Director need to make a career change?
- How do I translate self-reflection into a set of career goals?
- What are some typical career paths for former Executive Directors?

What are the first steps to making a career change?

The foundation for launching a new career emerges from an intentional process of self-reflection. The importance of this first step cannot be overemphasized. Whether you need a few hours or several months, it is important to be thorough and honest, and to take time to acknowledge your fears, self-doubts, passions, values, and gifts. A good place to start is to fully embrace your feelings about the job you are leaving—positive and negative—and use your past experience to inform your choice for the future. The inventory in Exhibit 19.1 will help to guide you, although it is by no means complete, and we urge you to follow the lead of other questions that may emerge and let the information you are gathering about yourself open you to new creative career possibilities.

What kind of support does an Executive Director need to make a career change?

The very nature of change is to push people beyond their comfort zones. Few would argue the value of support during significant life changes. Career change is indeed significant. Without question, a support system—formal or informal—is invaluable throughout the process.

Exhibit 19.1 Self-Reflection Inventory

- What do you enjoy most about your work? The compelling mission? The leadership role? The public persona? The day-to-day management?

- What responsibilities or relationships provide you with the greatest enjoyment?

- What responsibilities or relationships are the most frustrating for you?

- How do you feel about fundraising? Is it challenging? An inherent strength?

- Does partnering with the Board inspire or frustrate you?

- What will you miss most about your role as an ED? Visibility in the community? Your position of authority? Working with people?

- What do you need from your work? A living wage to support your family? Flexibility or balance in your life? Greater challenges?

You can build your support circle or team with friends, family, coworkers, or career professionals, as long as they are genuinely interested in you, will give you honest feedback, and be available to support and cheer you on. Given the common complaint that Executive Directors have few informal avenues for professional support, you may have to put some effort into developing a professional network. Whichever way you create your support system, it is important that you receive feedback from people who know you and have a broad array of experience and viewpoints to bring to your issues.

Wisdom

Look for opportunities in organizations with a culture that complements your own beliefs and values.

Story from the Field

Margaret has surrounded herself with three ongoing circles that each support different aspects of her career. Her first circle is her husband and sister, who both can be brutally honest while providing much-needed empathy and encouragement. Her second circle includes two other nonprofit Executive

Directors. They have worked together for nearly a decade, though their careers have taken radically different directions. They meet quarterly over breakfast to celebrate accomplishments, support challenges, and of course catch up on the news and trends in the field. Her third circle consists of four strong women who have thriving consulting practices. They push each other to envision and model consulting work as an extension of their values and expertise. One of the advantages of having these three sources of support is that it's relatively unlikely that meeting Margaret's needs will overburden any one circle.

Look around you. What are your current sources of support—and can they provide the insight and networking you need during this process? If not, are there structured career evaluation groups through your alumni association, church or synagogue, or local career development organization? Perhaps you need to invite a few people to lunch and create your own.

How do I translate self-reflection into a set of career goals?

Once you feel you have derived sufficient information from your self-reflection efforts, it is time to create a vision by creatively thinking about what you would like in a future career. By increasing focus on this vision, you will move beyond a vague dream to a more concrete reality of skills, values, and activities that you enjoy. Eventually you will step onto a more clearly defined career path with a set of goals. A good way to increase your focus is to put your thoughts down on paper and then ask the following questions:

- How will your life change if you achieve this vision or reach these goals?
- Do you like what you see?

Once you answer yes to the second question, share your vision with your support circle or network and ask them for feedback with regard to the following questions:

1. What are your thoughts about my vision and goals?
2. Have I overlooked anything?
3. How do my vision and goals translate into career opportunities?
4. Do any specific jobs or fields come to mind?

As you consider the feedback from your support network it is likely that one or more career possibilities will begin to come into focus. Take a look at where these possibilities will lead you in three to five years and then prepare to do some networking and research. Identify people already in these positions and make arrangements to talk with them and ask the following questions:

- What do you see as the strengths and challenges of your position?
- What does your typical work day or week look like?
- What skills and experience are your employers looking for?
- Do you know of any opportunities in this career path?
- Will you take a moment to review my résumé?
  Does my background look like a good fit?
  Do I need to retool my skills or my résumé to represent myself more effectively?

Frequently this kind of research and networking leads directly to your next job. When it doesn't, it is time to launch into an aggressive job search. Since this can be a full-time job in itself, it is important to be realistic about the time required and to pace yourself. Dedicate time each day or week to follow up on advertised openings. Be sure to continue to network and keep in contact

Wisdom

Be open to new ideas and fields of employment while remaining true to your professional gifts and needs.

Wisdom

Never underestimate the value of having a personal and professional support network available to you.

with your personal and professional support circles. These efforts will maximize your chances for a word-of-mouth contact that can land you the job that matches your personal and management values and offers you a culture that will allow you to maximize your experience and skills. The result should be a healthy yet balanced new career that you will love. You will prove to yourself that there is indeed life after being an Executive Director.

What are some typical career paths for former Executive Directors?

In our twenty years' experience in the field, we have observed some common paths that many former EDs pursue. The following ideas may help you match your interests and skills to a new career strategy.

Program Specialist or Director: If you find yourself driven by your organization's mission and love working closely with clients and their issues, consider stepping into a program role. Program management allows you to focus your energy and skills more directly on the heart of the mission rather than on balancing management and leadership roles.

Warning

Resist the temptation to settle for a job that compromises your vision and goals.

Development Director: Great fundraisers are great matchmakers. They have a special gift for matching community needs or an organization's vision with the investment resources of donors and community leaders. If you enjoy building and nurturing relationships with donors, designing outreach and community events, and are detail oriented in the context of tracking and recognizing donations, this may be the next job for you. Salaries for fundraisers with a proven track record in capital campaigns or planned giving are often comparable to those of Executive Directors.

Nonprofit Consultant: As a consultant, you can transfer your skills and expertise toward helping a variety of organizations. You can work independently or through a consulting firm. Consulting can provide great flexibility, but that flexibility may be counterbalanced by a lack of funds to sustain you as you build a practice, irregular paychecks, and fewer benefits. This field demands great time management and communication skills.

Interim management: Often organizations find themselves in need of an Executive Director or specialist to help with day-to-day management during staff transitions or sabbaticals. The primary differences between interim management and permanent positions are the length of service (usually a few months) and the scope of work (mostly internal and focused more on maintenance and support than innovation). You need to be able to hit the ground running, to quickly form relationships, and to gain the trust of the staff and the Board.

Government or public sector: The public and government sectors are similar to the nonprofit sector in the types of work done, accountability requirements, and work with Boards. In addition, this work normally includes night and weekend meetings and events. This may be a career opportunity if you are strong at consensus building and find the political arena intriguing. The benefits and retirement packages also tend to be very attractive.

Foundations: Your knowledge of the nonprofit sector and your experience raising funds can be transferred to the opportunities and challenges of grant making. Giving money isn't as easy as it may sound. Whether you are a Program Officer in a large foundation or a Director of a family fund, you need to be able to clearly define and articulate the organization's priorities while screening and prioritizing a multitude of requests and proposals. Many of these positions tend to be heavy on administration, while others are more externally focused.

Corporate sector, Community Affairs Officer: Many corporations feel strongly about their corporate responsibility to support the community in which they operate. Your experience in the nonprofit arena and

WARNING

If you think you haven't had enough time for self-reflection and research, don't rush to accept the first job opportunity that comes your way.

understanding of how to meet broader community needs are often directly transferable to a liaison post with a major corporation.

The message of this book is to support and sustain you in your career choice of Executive Director. While we hope that your current career is fulfilling, you may eventually want to leverage the incredible array of skills and relationships you have built into a new type of organization or even career path. Whatever your path, let your values and vision guide you to work that you love.

Conclusion

As you have surmised from this book, the role of an Executive Director is one of the biggest and most challenging jobs you will ever love. While the work itself is normally straightforward, the issues, relationships, competing priorities, and environment constantly change and scarcity demands incredible passion, focus, and leadership. It is not a career choice to be made lightly. And, once made, the choice of being an Executive Director is exciting and rewarding, as well as frustrating. For those Executive Directors who are committed to staying awhile longer in this incredible position, we commend you. We need you. Our hope is that *The Executive Director's Survival Guide* gives you new perspective and new tools for your leadership. Visit us often at edsurvivalguide.org for information, updates, resources, and advice to help you be more successful.

For those who are ready to move on to new careers, we thank you for bringing your passion to the profession. This book was inspired by those Executive Directors who have put passion before profit to make our neighborhoods, communities, and world a better place for all.

Resources

CHAPTER ONE

Books and Articles

Brinckerhoff, P. C. *Mission-Based Management: Leading Your Not-for-Profit into the 21st Century.* (2nd ed.) New York: Wiley, 2001.

Center for Nonprofit Management. *The Nonprofit Answer Book.* Los Angeles: Center for Nonprofit Management, 1998.

Connors, T. D. (ed.). *The Nonprofit Handbook: Management.* (3rd ed.) New York: Wiley, 2001.

De Pree, M. *Leading Without Power.* San Francisco: Jossey-Bass, 1997.

Drucker, P. *Managing the Non-Profit Organization.* New York: HarperCollins, 1990.

Gardner, J. W. *On Leadership.* New York: Free Press, 1990.

Greenleaf, R. *On Becoming a Servant Leader.* San Francisco: Jossey-Bass, 1996.

Hardy, J. M. *Managing for Impact in Nonprofit Organizations.* Erwin, Tex.: Essex Press, 1984.

Herman, R. D., and Associates. *Executive Leadership in Nonprofit Organizations.* San Francisco: Jossey-Bass, 1991.

Herman, R. D. (ed.). *The Jossey-Bass Handbook of Nonprofit Leadership and Management.* San Francisco: Jossey-Bass, 1994.

Hesselbein, F., Goldsmith, M., and Beckhard, R. (eds.). *Leader of the Future.* San Francisco: Jossey-Bass, 1996.

Kouzes, J., and Posner, B. *The Leadership Challenge.* (3rd ed.) San Francisco: Jossey-Bass, 2002.

Lewis, R. L. *Effective Nonprofit Management: Essential Lessons for Executive Directors.* New York: Aspen, 2001.

Nanus, B., and Dobbs, S. *Leaders Who Make a Difference.* San Francisco: Jossey-Bass, 1999.

National Assembly of National Voluntary Health and Social Welfare Organizations. *A Study in Excellence: Management in the Nonprofit Human Services.* Washington, D.C.: National Assembly of National Voluntary Health and Social Welfare Organizations, 1989.

Periodicals

Leader to Leader. Published quarterly by the Drucker Foundation and Jossey-Bass. Phone (888) 481-2665 or e-mail jbsubs@jbp.com for more information.

The Nonprofit Quarterly. Published by Third Sector New England of Boston, Massachusetts. Phone (800) 281-7770 or check http://www.nonprofitquarterly.org/ for more information.

NonProfit Times. Published by The Nonprofit Times, Parsippany, New Jersey. Phone (973) 394-1800 or fax (973) 394-2888 for more information; order on-line at http://www.nptimes.com/.

Online Resources

Note that Web sites and other online resources are subject to frequent change. All the URLs given here and in subsequent sections were active when we wrote this, but may not remain stable. If they don't take you to the expected site, try the organization or publication name in a search engine before assuming it's out of business.

Internet Nonprofit Center, http://www.nonprofits.org/.
Leader to Leader, http://www.leadertoleader.org/.

CHAPTER TWO

Books and Articles

Bennis, W. *On Becoming a Leader.* Reading, Mass.: Addison-Wesley, 1989.

Bennis, W., and Goldsmith, J. *Learning to Lead: A Workbook on Becoming a Leader.* Reading, Mass.: Addison-Wesley, 1994.

Kouzes, J. *Credibility: How Leaders Gain and Lose It, Why People Demand It.* San Francisco: Jossey-Bass, 1993.

Kouzes, J., and Posner, B. *Leadership Practices Inventory: A Self-Assessment and Analysis.* San Francisco: Jossey-Bass, 2001.

Kouzes, J., and Posner, B. *The Leadership Challenge: How to Keep Getting Extraordinary Things Done in Organizations.* (3rd ed.) San Francisco: Jossey-Bass, 2002.

Organizations

The following organizations provide management support to nonprofits. This is only a sample of organizations in each region that provide consulting, training, information resources or any combination of the three. For additional referrals, contact the Alliance for Nonprofit Management at http://www.allianceonline.org/ or your local United Way, Community Fund, or volunteer center. Any of the groups listed in the following sections may also be able to provide useful referrals.

West

Center for Excellence in Nonprofits, San Jose, California; http://www.cen.org/.

Center for Nonprofit Management in Southern California, Los Angeles, California; http://www.cnmsocal.org/.

Colorado Nonprofit Development Center, Denver, Co; http://www.startnonprofit.org/.

CompassPoint Nonprofit Services, San Francisco, California; http://www.compass point.org/.

East Bay Resource Center for Nonprofit Support, Oakland, California; http://www.info base.org/.

The Management Center, San Francisco, California ; http://www.tmc.org/.

Nonprofit Support Center of Santa Barbara County, Santa Barbara, California; http://www.nscsp.org/.

Sierra Nonprofit Support Center, Sonora, California; http://www.sierransc.org/.

Southwest

Arizona State University Center for Nonprofit Leadership and Management, Tempe, Arizona; http://www.asu.edu/copp/nonprofit.

Center for Nonprofit Management, Dallas, Texas; http://www.cnmdallas.org/.

Nonprofit Management Center of the Permian Basin, Midland, Texas; http://www.nmc-pb.org/.

Nonprofit Management Center of Wichita Falls, Wichita Falls, Texas.

Nonprofit Resource Center of Texas, San Antonio, Texas; http://www.nprc.org/.

Santa Fe Community Foundation, Santa Fe, New Mexico; http://www.santafecf.org/.

Midwest

Center for Management Assistance, Kansas City, Missouri; http://www.centersource.org/.

Center for Nonprofit Excellence, Akron, Ohio; http://www.cfnpe.org/.

Center for Nonprofit Management, Minneapolis, Minnesota; http://www.gsb.stthomas.edu/nonprofit.

Center for Nonprofits, Oklahoma City, Oklahoma; http://www.centerfornonprofits.us/.

Indiana Nonprofit Resource Network, Elkhart, Muncie, and Indianapolis, Indiana; http://www.iauw.org/.

Management Assistance Program for Nonprofits, St. Paul, Minnesota; http://www.mapfornonprofits.org/.

Mandel Center for Nonprofit Organizations, Cleveland, Ohio; http://www.cwru.edu/mandelcenter.

Michigan Nonprofit Association, Lansing, Michigan; http://www.mnaonline.org/.

Midwest Center for Nonprofit Leadership, Kansas City, Missouri; http://www.mcnl.org/.

Minnesota Council of Nonprofits, St. Paul, Minnesota; http://www.mncn.org/.

Nonprofit Alliance, Willard Public Library, Battle Creek, Michigan; http://www.willard.lib.mi.us/npa/.

Nonprofit Center of Milwaukee, Milwaukee, Wisconsin; http://www.execpc.com/npcm.

The Resource Center, Fargo, North Dakota; http://www.ndcf.net/.

University of Illinois at Chicago, Chicago, Illinois; http://www.cnm.cuppa.uic.edu/.

University of Michigan—Nonprofit & Public Management Center, Ann Arbor, Michigan; http://www.ssw.umich.edu/underoneroof.

Northeast

Bayer Center for Nonprofit Management, Pittsburgh, Pennsylvania; http://www.rmu.edu/bcnm.

BoardSource, Washington, D.C.; http://www.boardsource.org/.

Center for Nonprofit Services, Erie, Pennsylvania; http://www.cferie.org/.

LaSalle University Nonprofit Center, Philadelphia, Pennsylvania; http://www.lasallenonprofitcenter.org/.

Leader To Leader Institute, New York, New York; http://www.leadertoleader.org/.

Maryland Association of Nonprofit Organizations, Baltimore and Silver Springs, Maryland; http://www.mdnonprofit.org/.

National Council of Nonprofit Associations, Washington, D.C.; http://www.ncna.org/.

Nonprofit Leadership Institute, Pittsburgh, Pennsylvania; http://www.leadership.duq.edu/boardlink.

Not For Profit Resource Center, Buffalo, New York; http://www.uwbec.org/.

Support Center for Nonprofit Management, New York, New York, http://www.supportctr.org/.

York Nonprofit Management Development Center, York, Pennsylvania; http://www.ycp.edu/.

Southeast

C-One, Center on Nonprofit Effectiveness, Miami, Florida; http://www.c-one-miami.org/.

Center for Nonprofit Excellence, Louisville, KY; http://www.cnpe.org/.

Center for Nonprofit Management, Nashville, Tennessee; http://www.cnm.org/.

Center for Nonprofit Resources, New Orleans, Louisiana; http://www.nonprofit resources.org/.

Center for Nonprofits, Chattanooga, Tennessee; http://www.cnpchatt.org/.

Georgia Center for Nonprofits, Atlanta, Georgia; http://http://www.nonprofit georgia.org/.

Mississippi Center for Nonprofits, Jackson, Mississippi; http://www.msnonprofits.org/.

Nonprofit Center of Northeast Florida, Jacksonville, Florida; http://www.nonprofit jax.org/.

Nonprofit Resource Center, Sarasota, Florida; http://www.suncoastnonprofits.org/.

Nonprofit Resource Center of Alabama, Birmingham, Alabama; http://www.nrca.info.

Nonprofit Resource Institute of Palm Beach and Martin Counties, West Palm Beach, Florida; http://www.nonprofitinstitute.org/.

South Carolina Association of Nonprofit Organizations, Columbia, South Carolina; http://www.scanps.org/.

Periodical

Fast Company. Published by Gruner + Jahr USA Publishing. Phone (800) 542-6029 or check http://www.fastcompany.com/ for more information.

Online Resources

Coaches Training Institute; http://www.thecoaches.com/.

Directory of Life Coaches; http://www.lifecoachguide.com/.

Free Management Library, an online resource hosted by The Management Assistance Program, St. Paul, Minnesota; http://www.managementhelp.org; phone (651) 647-1216.

Institute for Professional Empowerment Coaching; http://www.ipeccoaching.com/.

International Coaches Federation; http://www.coachfederation.org/.

CHAPTER THREE

Books and Articles

Chambre, S. M. "Burnout: What to Do When You're at the End of Your Rope." *Volunteer Leadership,* July-Sept. 1998, pp. 23–24.

Corrigan, M. "Burnout: How to Spot It and Protect Yourself Against It." *Journal of Volunteer Administration,* Spring 1994, *12,* 24–31.

Covey, S. *The 7 Habits of Highly Effective People.* New York: Simon & Schuster, 1989.

Covey, S. *First Things First.* New York: Simon & Schuster, 1994.

Friedman, S. D., and Greenhaus, J. H. *Work-Family: Allies or Enemies?* Oxford, England: Oxford University PR on Demand, 2000.

Harari, O. *Leadership Secrets of Colin Powell.* Columbus, Ohio: McGraw-Hill, 2002.

Jenson, D. "In Search of the Balanced Leader." *Nonprofit World,* Nov.-Dec. 1998, *16,* 48–50.

Kofodimos, J. *Balancing Act: How Managers Can Integrate Successful Careers and Fulfilling Personal Lives.* San Francisco: Jossey-Bass, 1993.

Oncken, W., Jr., and Burrows, H. *The One Minute Manager Meets the Monkey.* New York: Morrow, 1989.

Weiss, A. *Life Balance: How to Convert Professional Success into Personal Happiness.* San Francisco: Jossey-Bass/Pfeiffer, 2003.

Online Resources

Balancing Act, an electronic newsletter discussing the blending of life, work, and relationships. Edited by Alan Weiss, Ph.D.; subscribe at balancingact@summit consulting.com.

The Free Management Library, hosted by the Management Assistance Program of St. Paul, Minnesota (see "Online Resources" for Chapter Two), has a Personal Wellness Page at http://www.managementhelp.org/prsn_wll/wrk_life.htm.

CHAPTER FOUR

Books and Articles

Bridges, W. *The Character of Organizations.* Palo Alto, Calif.: Davies-Black, 2000.

Harrison, R., and Stokes, H. *Diagnosing Organizational Culture.* San Francisco: Jossey-Bass, 1992.

Heskett, J. L., and Schlesinger, L. "Leaders Who Shape and Keep Performance-Oriented Culture," in F. Hesselbein, M. Goldsmith, and R. Beckhard, (eds.), *Leader of the Future.* San Francisco: Jossey-Bass, 1996.

Schein, E. *Organizational Culture and Leadership.* (2nd ed.) San Francisco: Jossey-Bass, 1992.

Online Resources

Management Strategies, Visionomics Quarterly Newsletter, http://www.vision omics.com/.

The Organizational Culture Web site, http://www.organizational-culture.com/.

Toolpack Consulting: Articles, http://www.toolpack.com/.

Other articles and newsletters can be found at http://www.leadershipadvantage.com/.

CHAPTER FIVE

Books and Articles

Allison, M., and Kaye, J. *Strategic Planning for Nonprofit Organizations*. New York: Wiley, 1997.

Barry, B. W. *The Strategic Planning Workbook for Nonprofit Organizations*. (2nd ed.) St. Paul, Minn.: Amherst H. Wilder Foundation, 2000.

Bryson, J. *Strategic Planning for Public and Nonprofit Organizations*. San Francisco: Jossey-Bass, 1993.

De Pree, M. *Leadership Is an Art*. New York: Doubleday, 1989.

Kouzes, J., and Posner, B. *The Leadership Challenge*. San Francisco: Jossey-Bass, 1995; see p. 95.

Nanus, B. *Visionary Leadership*. San Francisco: Jossey-Bass, 1992.

Schwartz, P. *The Art of the Long View*. New York: Doubleday, 1991.

CHAPTER SIX

Books and Articles

Carver, J. *CarverGuide: Board Assessment of the CEO*. San Francisco: Jossey-Bass, 1997.

Dees, J. G., Emerson, J., and Economy, P. *Strategic Tools for Social Entrepreneurs: Enhancing the Performance of your Enterprising Nonprofit*. New York: Wiley, 2002.

Drucker, P. F. "The Nonprofit Bottom Line." *NonProfit Times*, 1994, *8*, 44–45.

Dubois, A. "Is It Time for an Organizational Assessment?" *Nonprofit World*, 1995, *13*, 40, 42.

Fitz-Gibbon, C. T. *How to Design a Program Evaluation*. Thousand Oaks, Calif.: Sage, 1987.

Galer, D. "Achieving Quality in Nonprofits." *Nonprofit World*, 1988, *6*, 22–24.

Gray, S. T. *Evaluation with Power: A New Approach to Organizational Effectiveness, Empowerment, and Excellence*. San Francisco: Jossey-Bass, 1998.

Kibbee, B., and Setterberg, F. *Succeeding with Consultants: Self-Assessment for the Changing Nonprofit*. New York: Foundation Center, 1992.

Nanus, B., and Dobbs, S. *Leaders Who Make a Difference*. San Francisco: Jossey-Bass, 1999.

Pierson, J., and Mintz, J. *Assessment of the Chief Executive*. Washington, D.C.: BoardSource, 1999.

Stern, G. *The Drucker Foundation Self-Assessment Tool*. San Francisco: Jossey-Bass, 1999.

Temkin, T. "Evaluating the Executive Director, part 1 & 2," Fall 2002. Available online: Charity Channel Web Site, http://charitychannel.com/article_1351.shtml.

CHAPTER SEVEN

Books and Articles

Cavanagh, R., and Drucker, P. *Emerging Partnership: New Ways in a New World.* Available online: Leader to Leader Institute Web Site, http://leadertoleader.org/forms/partners.pdf.

Dees, J. G., Economy, P., Emerson, J., and Johnston, R. *Enterprising Nonprofits: A Toolkit for Social Entrepreneurs.* New York: Wiley, 2001.

Frumkin, P. "On Being Nonprofit: The Bigger Picture." *Harvard Business School Working Knowledge,* Sept. 9, 2002. Available online: http://leadertoleader.org/forms/4-99news.pdf.

Green, F. "10 Things Nonprofits Must Do in the 21st Century." *California Association of Nonprofits,* Jan.-Feb. 2000. Available online: http://www.CAnonprofits.org/.

"Insights from All Three Sectors." *Drucker Foundation News,* April 1999. Available online: http://leadertoleader.org/forms/4-99news.pdf.

"Job or Vocation." *Nonprofit Quarterly,* Feb. 2001, entire issue.

Light, P. *Making Nonprofits Work: A Report on the Tides Nonprofit Management Reform.* Washington, D.C.: Brookings Institution Press, 2000.

O'Neil, M. *Nonprofit Nation: A New Look at the Third America.* San Francisco: Jossey-Bass, 2002.

"Sector at Work: Identity Under Construction." *Nonprofit Quarterly,* July 2001, entire issue.

CHAPTER EIGHT

Books and Articles

Burns, M. "Act Your Age! The Organizational Lifecycle and How It Affects Your Board." *Nonprofit Quarterly,* Summer 1997. Available online: http://216.65.35.60/pdf/actyourage.pdf.

Franco, N., Gross, S., and Mathiasen, K. "Organizational Life Cycles: Preparing Your Organization For Evolution." Washington D.C.: Planning and Management Assistance Project, 1992.

Greiner, L. "Evolution and Revolution as Organizations Grow." *Harvard Business Review,* May-June 1998, 55–68. (Originally published in the Jul.-Aug. 1972 issue.)

Hernandez, C. M., and Leslie, D. R. "Charismatic Leadership: The Aftermath." *Nonprofit Management & Leadership,* 2001, *11,* 493–497.

McLaughlin, T. A. "Where Is Your Agency? The Life Cycle of Nonprofit Organizations." *Nonprofit Times,* 1996, *10,* 27.

Miller, L. *Barbarians to Bureaucrats.* New York: Potter, 1989.

Quinn, R. E., and Cameron, K. "Organizational Life Cycles and Some Shifting Criteria of Effectiveness." *Management Science,* 1983, *29,* 31–51.

Simon, J. S., and Donovan, J. T. *The Five Life Stages of Nonprofit Organizations.* Saint Paul, Minn.: Amherst H. Wilder Foundation, 2001.

CHAPTER NINE

Books and Articles

Black, J. S., and Gregersen, H. B. *Leading Strategic Change.* Upper Saddle River, N.J.: Prentice Hall, 2002.

Dolny, H. *Banking On Change.* London: Viking Press, 2001.

Duck, J. D. *The Change Monster.* New York: Random House, 2001.

Dyck, B. "The Role of Crises and Opportunities in Organizational Change: A Look at a Nonprofit Religious College." *Nonprofit and Voluntary Sector Quarterly,* Sept. 1996, *25,* 321–346.

Eadie, D. C. *Changing by Design: A Practical Approach to Leading Innovation in Nonprofit Organizations.* San Francisco: Jossey-Bass, 1997.

Fullan, M. *Leading in a Culture of Change.* San Francisco: Jossey-Bass, 2001.

Galaskiewicz, J., and Bielefeld, W. *Nonprofit Organizations in an Age of Uncertainty: A Study of Organizational Change.* Hawthorne, N.Y.: Aldine de Gruyter, 1998.

Grobman, G. M. *Improving Quality and Performance in your Non-Profit Organization: An Introduction to Change Management Strategies for the 21st Century.* Harrisburg, Pa.: White Hat Communications, 1999.

Johnson, S. *Who Moved My Cheese?* New York: Putnam, 1998.

Kotter, J. P. "Winning at Change." *Leader to Leader,* 1998, *10,* 27–33.

Letts, C. *High Performance Nonprofit Organizations: Managing Upstream for Greater Impact.* New York: Wiley, 1998.

Online Resources

The HRD Group Ltd., Nottingham, England; http://www.organisationalchange.co.uk.

Interchange International, Dallas, Texas; phone (800) 878-8422; http://www.change cycle.com/.

Maurer & Associates; phone (703) 525-7074; http://www.beyondresistance.com/.

CHAPTER TEN

Books and Articles

Bell, P. D. *Fulfilling The Public's Trust: Ten Ways to Help Nonprofit Boards Maintain Accountability.* Washington, D.C.: National Center For Nonprofit Boards, 1993.

Carver, J. *Boards That Make a Difference.* San Francisco: Jossey-Bass, 1997.

Carver, J. *CarverGuides.* (Twelve Pamphlets For Board Members). San Francisco: Jossey-Bass, 1997.

Chait, R. P. *How to Help Your Board Govern More and Manage Less.* Washington D.C.: National Center For Nonprofit Boards, 1993.

Connor, J. A., and Kadel-Taras, S. "Governing Outside: Bringing the Board Into the Community." *Board Member,* 2000, *9,* 6–7.

Herman, R. D., and Heimovics, R. D. *Executive Leadership in Nonprofit Organizations.* San Francisco: Jossey-Bass, 1991.

Houle, C. O. *Governing Boards: Their Nature and Nurture.* San Francisco: Jossey-Bass, 1989.

Hughes, S., Lakey, B., and Bobowick, M. *The Board Building Cycle: Nine Steps to Finding, Recruiting, and Engaging Nonprofit Board Members.* Washington, D.C.: BoardSource, 2000.

Jackson, D. K., and Holland, T. P. "Measuring the Effectiveness of Nonprofit Boards." *Nonprofit and Voluntary Sector Quarterly,* 1998, *27.*

Leifer, J. C., and Glomb, M. B. *The Legal Obligations of Nonprofit Boards: A Guidebook for Board Members.* Washington, D.C. National Center for Nonprofit Boards, 1997.

Nelson, J. G. *Six Keys to Recruiting, Orienting, and Involving Nonprofit Board Members.* Washington, D.C.: National Center for Nonprofit Boards, 1991.

O'Connell, B. *Board Overboard: Laughs and Lessons for All but the Perfect Nonprofit.* San Francisco: Jossey-Bass, 1995.

Souccar, M. K. "Lunching Ladies Meet Hip-Hop: A Charity Finds New Donors, Vitality." *Crain's New York Business,* May 2002, *18.*

Szanton, P. L. *Board Assessment of the Organization: How Are We Doing?* Washington, D.C.: National Center for Nonprofit Boards, 1992.

Taylor, B. E., Chait, R. P., and Holland, T. P. "The New Work of the Nonprofit Board." *Harvard Business Review,* Sept.-Oct., 1996. Reprint #96509.

Walsh, J. A. "Nonprofit Boards: Eight Leadership Development Stories." *Nonprofit World,* 2002, *20*(1), 11–17.

Wood, M. N. (ed.). *Nonprofit Boards and Leadership: Cases on Governance, Change, and Board-Staff Dynamics.* San Francisco: Jossey-Bass, 1996.

Organizations

BoardSource, Washington, D.C.; phone (800) 883-6262; http://www.boardsource.org/.

Trustee Leadership Development, Indianapolis, Indiana; phone (877) 564-6853; http://www.tld.org/.

Periodicals

Board Leadership: Policy Governance in Action, edited by J. Carver. Published bimonthly by Jossey-Bass. Phone (888) 378-2537 for more information.

Board Member. Published bimonthly by BoardSource. Phone (800) 883-6262 or check http://www.boardsource.org/ for more information.

CHAPTER ELEVEN

Books and Articles

De Pree, M. *Leading Without Power*. San Francisco: Jossey-Bass, 1997.

Hacker, C. A. *The High Cost of Low Morale*. Boca Raton, Fla.: Saint Lucie Press, 1997.

Kouzes, J., and Posner, B. *Encouraging the Heart*. San Francisco: Jossey-Bass, 1999.

Messmer, M. *Human Resources Kit for Dummies*. Foster City, Calif.: IDG Books Worldwide, 1999.

Rees, F. *Teamwork from Start to Finish*. San Francisco: Jossey-Bass/Pfeiffer, 1997.

Senge, P. *The Fifth Discipline: The Art and Practice of the Learning Organization*. New York: Doubleday, 1990.

Weisbord, M. *Productive Workplaces: Organizing and Managing for Dignity, Meaning, and Community*. San Francisco: Jossey-Bass, 1987.

CHAPTER TWELVE

Books and Articles

Adams, T. "Departing? Arriving? Surviving and Thriving Lessons for Executives." *Nonprofit Quarterly,* Winter 2003, p. 6.

Block, S., and Rosenburg, S. "Toward an Understanding of Founder's Syndrome." *Nonprofit Management and Leadership,* Summer 2002, p. 353.

Clampa, D., and Watkins, M. "The Successor's Dilemma." *Harvard Business Review,* Nov.-Dec. 1999.

Lewis, H. "Founder's Syndrome: An Affliction for Which There Is Rarely Immunity." Charity Channel Governance Review, June 27, 2002. Available online: http://charity channel.com/article_26.shtml.

McNamara, C. *Founder's Syndrome: How Corporations Suffer and Can Recover*. St. Paul, Minn.: Management Assistance Program for Nonprofits, 1999. Available online: http://www.managementhelp.org/misc/founders.htm.

Rechtman, J. "Legacy and Letting Go: A Framework for Leadership Transfer." *Board Source,* April 2000, p. 8.

Redington, E., and Vickers, D. *Following the Leaders: A Guide for Planning Founding Director Transition*. Columbus, Ohio: Academy for Leadership and Governance, 2001.

CHAPTER THIRTEEN

Books and Articles

Bonk, K., Griggs, H., and Tynes, E. *The Jossey-Bass Guide to Strategic Communications for Nonprofits.* San Francisco: Jossey-Bass, 2002.

Elberg, G., and Phillips, J. "The Art of Community Building in Light of R. Putnam's *Bowling Alone." Journal of Volunteer Administration,* 2001, *19*(3), 33.

Etling, A. "Evaluability Assessment Clarifies Complex Programs." *Journal of Volunteer Administration,* 1990, *8*(3), 21–28.

Ferguson, S. D. *Mastering the Public Opinion Challenge.* New York: McGraw-Hill, 1993.

Kirkman, L., and Loeb, R. *Center for Strategic Communications: Introduction Volume-Strategic Communications for Nonprofits.* Washington, D.C.: Benton Foundation, 1992.

Mattessich, P. W., Monsey, B. R., and Roy, C. *Community Building: What Makes It Work—A Review of Factors Influencing Successful Community Building.* St. Paul, Minn.: Amherst H. Wilder Foundation, 1997.

Radtke, J. M. *Strategic Communications for Nonprofit Organizations: Seven Steps to Creating a Successful Plan.* New York: Wiley, 1998.

CHAPTER FOURTEEN

Books and Articles

Arsenault, J. *Forging Nonprofit Alliances.* San Francisco: Jossey-Bass, 1998.

Austin, J. *The Collaboration Challenge.* San Francisco: Jossey-Bass, 2000.

Bergquist, W., Betwee, J., and Meuel, D. *Building Strategic Relationships: How to Extend Your Organization's Reach Through Partnerships, Alliances, and Joint Ventures.* San Francisco: Jossey-Bass, 1995.

"Building Strategic Partnerships." *Nonprofit Quarterly,* Fall 2001, entire issue.

Buono, A. F., and others. "When Cultures Collide: The Anatomy of a Merger." *Human Relations,* 1983, *38*(5), 447–500.

Golensky, M., and DeRuiter, G. L. "The Urge to Merge: A Multiple-Case Study." *Nonprofit Management & Leadership,* 2002, *13*, 137.

James Irvine Foundation. "Strategic Solutions: Mergers and Acquisitions Nonprofit Style." *Irvine Quarterly,* Summer 2002.

La Piana, D. *Nonprofit Mergers: The Board's Responsibility to Consider the Unthinkable.* Washington D.C.: National Center for Nonprofit Boards, 1994.

La Piana, D. *Beyond Collaboration: Strategic Restructuring of Nonprofit Organizations.* Washington D.C.: National Center for Nonprofit Boards, 1997.

La Piana, D. *The Nonprofit Mergers Handbook: Leader's Guide to Considering, Negotiating, and Executing a Merger.* St. Paul, Minn.: Amherst H. Wilder Foundation, 2000.

Mattessich, P., Murray-Close, M., and Monsey, B. *Collaboration: What Makes It Work.* (2nd ed.) St. Paul, Minn.: Amherst H. Wilder Foundation, 2001.

Wheeler, D. "Rethinking Nonprofit Partnerships." *Chronicle of Philanthropy,* June 27, 2002.

Online Resources

"Collaborations: What Makes It Work," workshops from the Leader to Leader Institute, http://www.leadertoleader.org/.

"Emerging Partnerships: New Ways in a New World," Leader to Leader Institute Reports, http://www.leadertoleader.org/.

"Meeting the Collaboration " a monthly e-mail newsletter from the Leader to Leader Institute Challenge, http://www.leadertoleader.org/.

Strategic Solutions, http://www.lapiana.org/.

CHAPTER FIFTEEN

Books and Articles

Digh, R. "Culture? What Culture?" *Association Management,* 2001, *53.*

Digh, R. "Developing a Diversity Statement." *Association Management,* 1999, *51,* 53–55.

Elmes, M. B., and Prasad, P. *Managing the Organizational Melting Pot: Dilemmas of Workplace Diversity.* Thousand Oaks, Calif.: Sage, 1997.

Gardenswartz, L. *The Managing Diversity Survival Guide.* New York: McGraw-Hill, 1994.

Glasrud, B. "Beyond Diversity." *Nonprofit World,* 2000, *18*(2).

Gough, S. N., Jr. *Five Reasons for Nonprofit Organizations to Be Inclusive.* New Directions for Philanthropic Fundraising, no. 34. San Francisco: Jossey-Bass, 2001.

Hesselbein, F., Goldsmith, A., and Somerville, I. *Leading Beyond the Walls: How High-Performing Organizations Collaborate for Shared Success.* San Francisco: Jossey-Bass, 2001.

Roosevelt, T., Jr. *Beyond Race and Gender: Unleashing the Power of Your Total Work Force by Managing Diversity.* New York: AMACOM, 1991.

Seagel, S., and Horne, D. *Human Dynamics: A New Framework for Understanding People and Realizing the Potential in our Organizations.* Waltham, Mass.: Pegasus Communications, 2000.

Sidberry, T. B. "Building Diversity in Organizations." *Nonprofit Quarterly,* 2002, *9*(2).

Tannen, D. *You Just Don't Understand: Women and Men in Conversation.* New York: Ballantine, 1990.

Williams, M. A. and Clifton., D. O. *The 10 Lenses: Your Guide to Living and Working in a Multicultural World.* Herndon, Va.: Capital Books, 2001.

Zhu, J., and Kleiner, B. "The Failure of Diversity Training." *Nonprofit World,* 2000, *18*(3).

Online Resources

About.com is searchable for a number of diversity issues; http://humanresources.about.com/.

Diversity and Ethnic Studies—Recommended Web Sites and Research Guides, developed by S. A. Vega Garcia of Iowa State University; http://www.public.iastate.edu/~savega/divweb2.htm.

CHAPTER SIXTEEN

Books and Articles

Dropkin, M., and LaTouche, B. *The Budget-Building Book for Nonprofits: A Step-by-Step Guide for Managers and Boards.* San Francisco: Jossey-Bass, 1998.

"Financial Str(u/i)ctures." *Nonprofit Quarterly,* Spring 2003, entire issue.

Larkin, R. F. *Wiley GAAP Not-for-Profit Field Guide 2003.* New York: Wiley, 2003.

Sumariwalla, R. D., and Levis, W. C. *Unified Financial Reporting System for Not-for-Profit Organizations.* San Francisco: Jossey-Bass, 2000.

Online Resources

Genie (a series of FAQs on finance topics including audit, Form 990, and fiscal sponsorship); http://www.genie.com/.

Guidestar (an easy-to-use Web site that allows you to search for the Form 990 filed by any nonprofit organization); http://www.guidestar.com/.

CHAPTER SEVENTEEN

Books and Articles

Carlson, M. *Team-Based Fundraising: Step by Step.* San Francisco: Jossey-Bass, 2000.

Grace, K. S. *Beyond Fundraising: New Strategies For Nonprofit Innovation and Investment.* New York: Wiley, 1997.

Joyaux, S. P. *Strategic Fund Development.* New York: Aspen, 1997.

Klein, K. *Fundraising for Social Change.* Oakland, Calif.: Chardon Press, 2001.

Klein, K. *Fundraising for the Long Haul.* Oakland, Calif.: Chardon Press, 2001.

Rees, F. *Teamwork from Start to Finish.* San Francisco: Jossey-Bass, 1997.

Rosso, H. A., and Associates. *Achieving Excellence in Fundraising.* San Francisco: Jossey-Bass, 1991.

Schaff, T., and Schaff, D. *The Fundraising Planner.* San Francisco: Jossey-Bass, 1999.

CHAPTER EIGHTEEN

Books and Articles

Angowski, L. *Time Off from Work: Using Sabbaticals to Enhance your Life While Keeping your Career on Track.* New York: Wiley, 1994.

Axelrod, N. *Chief Executive Succession Planning: The Board's Role in Securing Your Organization's Future.* Washington, D.C.: BoardSource, 2002.

Bridges, W. *The Way of Transition: Embracing Life's Most Difficult Moments.* Cambridge, Mass.: Perseus, 2001.

Bridges, W. *Managing Transitions: Making the Most of Change.* Cambridge, Mass.: Perseus, 2003.

Dlugzima, H. *Six Months Off: How to Plan, Negotiate, and Take the Break You Need without Burning Bridges or Going Broke.* New York: Henry Holt, 1996.

"Leadership Transition: Critical Thresholds." *Nonprofit Quarterly,* Winter 2002, entire issue.

Managing Executive Transitions: A Handbook for Nonprofit Organizations. Washington, D.C.: Neighborhood Reinvestment Corporation, 1994.

Rechtman, J. *Legacy and Letting Go: A Framework for Leadership Transfer.* Washington, D.C.: National Center for Nonprofit Boards, 2000.

Wolfred, T. *Leadership Lost.* San Francisco: CompassPoint Nonprofit Services, 1998.

Wolfred, T. *Daring to Lead: Studies of Executive Director Tenure and Experience.* San Francisco: CompassPoint Nonprofit Services, 2001.

Zahorski, K. *The Sabbatical Mentor: A Practical Guide to Successful Sabbaticals.* Bolton, Mass.: Anker, 1994.

Online Resource

Tips for Turning a Vacation into a Mini-Sabbatical; http://www.IvySea.com/.

CHAPTER NINETEEN

Books and Articles

Albion, M. *Finding Work That Matters* (audiocassette). Louisville, Colo.: Sounds True, 2002.

Bolles, R. N. *What Color Is Your Parachute: A Practical Manual for Job-Hunters and Career-Changers.* Berkeley, Calif.: Ten Speed Press, 2002.

Sher, B. *I Could Do Anything If I Only Knew What It Was.* New York: DTP, 1995.

Online Resources

Career Center; http://www.Monster.com/.

Career Zones; http://www.Fastcompany.com/.

Richard Noelsen Bolles' Web site; Jobhuntersbible.com/.

Organizations

Association of Fundraising Professionals (AFP); http://www.afpnet.org/.

Council for Advancement and Support of Education (CASE); http://www.case.org/.

The Foundation Center—Cooperating Collections Throughout the United States; http://www.fdncenter.org/.

Periodicals

Advancing Philanthropy. Published bimonthly by the AFP. See http://www.afpnet.org/ for more information.

Chronicle of Philanthropy: The Newspaper of the Non-Profit World. Published biweekly. See http://www.philanthropy.com/ for more information.

Index

organizational life cycle stages, 81–84; staff relationships of, 119–132; staying inspired as, 21–23; succeeding as, 3–12; susceptibility of, to burnout, 26–27; work plan for, 105, 107–108, 111

Executive Director, new: Board Chair relationship with, 113; Founder transition management and, 133–141; staff relationships with, 120–123, 126–128; timing of organizational change process for, 91–92

Executive Director's Guide (Linnell, Radosevich, and Spack), 95

Exit strategy, 211–218

Expansion and growth stage, 79; Executive Director skills for, 83; fundraising in, 199

Expectations: decision-making authority and, 111; sharing, with Board Chair, 113, 115; unreasonable or unrealistic, 27, 63

Expense accounting, 182–183

External stakeholders. *See* Stakeholders, external

F

Family health community clinic, case story, 10–11

Farquharson, P., 93

Feasibility studies, 60

Feedback: for career transition, 221, 223; e-mail and, 131; on Executive Director effectiveness, 64–66; openness to, as criterion for organizational effectiveness, 62; from renegade Board members, 116; from staff, 127, 129–130. *See also* Communication

Financial analysis, 180

Financial management, 177, 179–193; accountability for, 179; budgeting and, 180, 184, 187–189; fiscal year in, 193; key activities of, 180; key issues of, 179–180; nonprofit *versus* for-profit, 181–183; resources on, 242–243; roles and responsibilities in, 183–188

Financial monitoring: misappropriation of funds and, 189–190; responsibility for, 186, 191, 193

Financial reports, 109, 180, 190–193; communication chart for, 192; fiscal year determination for, 193; frequency of, 191, 192; informational requirements of, 190–191, 192; roles and responsibilities for, 185–186; types of, 192

Finding Work That Matters (Albion), 219

Fiscal year, 193

Fit, 43–44

Ford, H., 177

Former Board members, 151

Foundation careers, 225

Founders, 133–141; Board effectiveness and, 101–102, 134–135; as Board members, 135–137; challenges of, 134–135; as consultants, 138–141; definition of, 133–134; emeritus status for, 137; emotional reactions of, 133–134, 138; as Executive Directors, 139–140; key issues of, 134; organizational culture based on, 41, 43, 46; problematic, 137–138, 139–141; relationships with, 133–141; resources for transition of, 239–240; roles for, 136–137, 141; as staff members, 138–141; transitional period with, 134–135

Founder's Syndrome, 133

Franco, N., 77

Fraud, 189–190

Friendship, 131–132

Functional expenses, 182–183

Fund development status reports, 109

Fund misappropriation, 189–190

Funders: communication with, 150, 192; pressures for collaboration and, 157. *See also* Donors

Fundraising, 177, 195–203; culture for, 196–198, 201–203; expense accounting for, 183; goal setting for, 201–202; information system for, 201, 202, 203; key activities of, 198; key issues of, 195–196; for overhead expenses, 200–203; performance goals for, 108; resources on, 243; responsibilities matrix for, 197; roles and responsibilities in, 196–198; team-